HISTORY'S MYSTERIES

LEGENDS AND LORE

CURIOUS CLUES, COLD CASES, AND PUZZLES FROM THE PAST

ANNA CLAYBOURNE

NATIONAL GEOGRAPHIC

WASHINGTON, D.C.

CONTENTS

RUINS OF THE
KOM OMBO TEMPLE IN EGYPT

A jötunn, a type of giant
from Norse mythology

INTRODUCTION

IF THERE'S ONE THING we humans love, it's a great story. In every culture, there are old, strange, and supernatural stories: myths and legends, folktales, fairy tales, and ancient accounts of how the world began. Besides being passed from person to person, they are shown in artworks, painted onto pottery, and carved into buildings. But where do they come from? Are they made up, or could they be based on reality?

Perhaps some of those old stories hold clues to things that happened in history—like ancient inventions, incredible creatures that once existed ... or even, according to some theories, evidence that aliens visited our planet in the past.

Step inside the pages of this book and you'll find buried treasures and magical maps, eyewitness accounts of dragons and mermaids, and mysterious ruins that could be the real-life locations of famous legends.

These mythical mysteries have continued into more recent history, too. Did a palace guard magically teleport across the world? What happened to the vanishing lighthouse keepers, the explorers who disappeared into the jungle, and Mount Everest's missing mountaineers? The supernatural stories and strange rumors that swirl around these events make them even more murky and mind-boggling. This book is here to explore the mysteries, uncover the history, and crack the curious clues ... in the hope that someday, someone—maybe you!—might find the answers.

ANCIENT ROCK ART IN KIMBERLEY, AUSTRALIA, SHOWING WANDJINAS, OR CREATOR BEINGS

People once thought dragons were real. But why did they think that?

7

FABLES AND FOLKLORE

An illustration from around A.D. 1850 depicting the building of Rama's bridge

THROUGHOUT HISTORY, people have sat around the
fire and told each other traditional tales.
Sometimes those tales belong to one particular
culture or place. But other times, they seem
oddly similar to others told around the world. These
tales of old are nothing more than stories told at
bedtime to help children nod off to sleep.

Or are they? What if those strange old stories,
however magical and impossible they might seem,
were actually based on real-life events—events that
happened so long ago that the truth has been
obscured by the mists of time? Of course, folktales
like these are nothing more than old stories, passed
down from person to person over the centuries.

RAMA'S BRIDGE

DID HUMANS BUILD AN ANCIENT BRIDGE ACROSS THE SEA?

THE BACKGROUND

THE ANCIENT INDIAN POEM the *Ramayana* is a Hindu epic that tells how the wife of the great god Rama was kidnapped by a demon king. The evil ruler takes her across the sea to his domain, Lanka. To get her back, Rama must cross the ocean. So he recruits an army of Vanara, often depicted as monkey-like men, to throw rocks into the sea until they form a bridge to reach Lanka.

This tale is a myth, but it's set in real places. Lanka is actually Sri Lanka, an island in South Asia. In satellite photos, you can see a 20-mile (32-km) string of islands and reefs stretching from Sri Lanka to India, like a string of stepping-stones. In some spots, they're connected by sandbars. Is this the "bridge" that Rama and his army built? Some think it is, and that rising seas over the past centuries have now partly hidden the ancient walkway underwater.

ASIA

INDIA

SRI LANKA

INDIA

Bay of Bengal

Rama's Bridge

SRI LANKA

INDIAN OCEAN

An army of monkey-like men constructing the bridge

The **RAMAYANA** is a superlong epic poem: It has **24,000** verses.

AN AERIAL VIEW OF ONE END OF RAMA'S BRIDGE TODAY

THE DETAILS

THE BRIDGE— or the chain of islands—between India and Sri Lanka is about 30 miles (50 km) long. That's a big bridge to build, even by today's standards. In fact, the world's longest continuous bridge over water, the Lake Pontchartrain Causeway in Louisiana, U.S.A., isn't even that long: It's just under 24 miles (38 km). In ancient times, it would have been a huge engineering feat to find and move enough rocks to make a causeway this long, and it would also have taken an incredibly long time. Some say it would have been impossible— except, of course, for a god like Rama, who had supernatural powers.

THE CLUES
Geologists have studied the bridge to try to find out if it's natural or not. There are also clues from historical records that tell us more about the bridge's past.

SAND SECRETS In 2007, a team of geologists drilled into the shallow seabed at Rama's Bridge to see what it was made of. They found rocky boulders and chunks on top of a layer of sand: the opposite of normal seafloor composition.

A WORKING BRIDGE Some descriptions from history say the bridge was a solid causeway that people could walk across. According to records kept in a temple on the Indian side of the bridge, it was broken by a storm in the year 1480.

X MARKS THE SPOT Rama's Bridge can also be found on several old maps, looking much more substantial than it is today. It's often shown as a raised track that would have appeared at low tide.

THE VANARA FROM THE STORY OF RAMA'S BRIDGE

RAMA'S BRIDGE IN A SATELLITE IMAGE

THE THEORIES

In this picture you can see the army of Vanara, or men depicted as monkeys.

THE MORE EXPERTS INVESTIGATE Rama's Bridge, the more they disagree and argue. For those who say it was built by humans, the layers of rock and large chunks of coral on top of sand are proof. They claim it was just a natural sandy seabed to start with, until someone deliberately piled the coral on top.

Wrong! says the other side. Some scientists claim natural forces such as currents, tsunamis, or typhoons could have deposited the boulders. They say it's also possible that Rama's Bridge is a tombolo, a strip of sand that forms naturally as waves travel sideways along a shoreline and connects an island to the mainland. As the old maps show, Rama's Bridge was once more solid, and it has been partly covered up or washed away by rising sea levels. It's possible that ancient people could have added rocks on top of this natural bridge to make it stronger. Instead of building the whole thing from scratch, perhaps they got a little help from nature.

If humans really did build some kind of bridge here, who were they? They could have been ancient Indian or Sri Lankan people who lived a few thousand years ago. But based on some Hindu beliefs, the god Rama lived more than a million years ago, so that's when the bridge would have been built, according to the legend. It's hard to see how, as modern humans didn't exist then!

But hang on a minute! Didn't the old poem say that Rama's army of Vanara, or monkey-like forest people, moved the stones? Believers say that fits perfectly—since the humans who lived over a million years ago were exactly that: our smaller, more monkey-like ancestors! It's a neat explanation, but scientists don't think these early humans could really have achieved such a feat. Were prehistoric people smarter than we thought ... or is this just a lot of monkey business?

THE PIED PIPER

DOES THIS FAMOUS FAIRY TALE HIDE A TERRIBLE TRUTH?

THE BACKGROUND

YOU'VE PROBABLY HEARD the tale of the Pied Piper of Hamelin. This old German legend has been turned into children's books and cartoons, films, and even a ballet. Which is weird, because if you think about it, the story is pretty scary! According to the legend, in 1284, more than 700 years ago, the town of Hamelin, Germany, was infested with a plague of rats. When an odd-looking visitor in a colorful outfit offered to get rid of them for a fee, the townspeople gratefully agreed. The stranger played a magical tune on his pipe, luring all the rats into the river. But once they saw how easy it was, the tightfisted townsfolk refused to pay up! In revenge, the Piper returned a few days later, played his pipe again ... and this time, he lured away all the town's children. They disappeared into a mountainside and were never seen again. Yikes! Even creepier, the tale seems to be based on real events. Historical records suggest that Hamelin's children really did vanish—in that very year! What happened to them?

North Sea

NETH.

POLAND

Hamelin

GERMANY

BELG.

CZECH REP.

FRANCE

SWITZ.

GERMANY

ASIA

EUROPE

AFRICA

Hamelin was a grain trading town with a lot of **FLOUR MILLS,** so rat **INFESTATIONS** were common.

The Piper charms away the rats in an old illustration of the story.

THE DETAILS

ONE OF THE BEST KNOWN versions of the tale is an 1842 poem by English writer Robert Browning. He included lots of details about the rats, and at the end, he described the children being led inside the magical mountain.

○────────○

When, lo, as they reached the mountain-side
A wondrous portal opened wide,
As if a cavern was suddenly hollowed;
And the Piper advanced and the children
followed,
And when all were in to the very last,
The door in the mountain-side shut fast.

○────────○

But it's not all that accurate. Browning helped popularize the creepy tale, and many modern versions are based on his poem. But if you go further back and look at the historical accounts, the story changes. In early reports, there are no rats at all—just the children being led away and lost.

THE CLUES
In the town of Hamelin itself, you can find several curious clues about the legend dating back hundreds of years.

A MODERN STAINED GLASS WINDOW DEPICTING THE PIED PIPER

SPOOKY STAINED GLASS
In about 1300, not long after the legend says the children disappeared, the town had a new stained glass window made for its central church that told the story. The window was later replaced, but paintings that depict the original have survived, showing the Piper with his colorful suit and pipe, the crowd of children, and the mountain in the distance.

THE WRITING ON THE WALL
Hamelin also has a building called the Rattenfängerhaus (Ratcatcher's House), which has an inscription on the side describing the disappearance. It reads (translated from German):

A.D. 1284—on the 26th of June—the day of St. John and St. Paul—130 children—born in Hamelin—were led out of the town by a piper wearing multicolored clothes. After passing the calvary near the Koppen hill they disappeared forever.

CLUES IN THE CHRONICLES
Old manuscripts and town history records from the local area mention the events. They specify a date of June 26, 1284, describe the Piper's colorful clothes, and say that 130 children went with him. Some add that they vanished at a hill called the Koppen.

THE THEORIES

THE MYSTERY IS SO INTRIGUING, scholars have spent years trying to figure out what really happened. They've come up with several theories—but which one is true?

Some say the Piper in the story might not be a real person but a symbol for death. Around that time, many people died from common diseases; perhaps a wave of measles or scarlet fever had hit the town? Other people think the children could have been lost in a cave or buried by a landslide. That would explain the part about the mountain swallowing them up.

But the most convincing theory is that the children left willingly to start new lives. It turns out that in the 1200s, many poor people from this part of Germany moved east, to what is now Poland, to work for landowners there. The landowners sent recruiters to German towns to offer jobs to young people—and they were said to wear bright clothes and play music to get everyone's attention. Today, some experts believe the "children" in the poem were actually teenagers, tempted by the promise of a brighter future. As they left, they would have passed through a hillside village called Coppenbrügge—perhaps that's the "Koppen hill" where they disappeared.

The townspeople may have memorialized the event in inscriptions, songs, and poetry. But if this theory is right, perhaps the children not only survived the experience but in fact went off to lead a better life. That would make the truth much happier than the fairy tale!

Art showing the children being led into the mountain by the Pied Piper

1 7

THE GREAT FLOOD

DID A **DISASTROUS** DELUGE *REALLY* DROWN THE WORLD?

YU THE GREAT IS SAID TO HAVE TAMED THE YELLOW RIVER.

If Earth were the size of a **BASKETBALL** all its water would fit into a space smaller than a **PING-PONG BALL.**

The animals wait to enter the Ark, in a painting of the Bible story of Noah.

THE BACKGROUND

A HUGE FLOOD covering all the land in the world and drowning all the people and animals ... except for a lucky few. Sound familiar? Wherever you come from, you'll probably know an old flood story like this.

The Christian Bible includes a famous version of the story: Noah's Ark. God tells Noah to build a boat—the Ark—that he, his family, and two of each animal can board to escape from the flood that is about to engulf the world. And there are hundreds of other spookily similar flood stories in myths, legends, and ancient books from around the globe.

In "The Epic of Gilgamesh," an ancient Sumerian poem, the gods decide to destroy the world with a flood. The god Ea warns a man named Utnapishtim to build a boat to save a few people, animals, and seeds. In Greek mythology, Zeus sends a mighty flood, and only one lucky couple, Deucalion and Pyrrha, survive. In Hindu legends, the god Vishnu appears as a fish to Manu, the first man, to warn him that a great flood is coming.

In China, there's the legend of the great Yellow River flood, which swept away everyone except one man, Yu, and his turtle. There are great floods in Native American, African, and Australian Aboriginal stories, too. People in these far-apart places couldn't contact each other back then, so these flood stories seem to have arisen independently. Maybe that means they're not just stories. Did a huge flood put the world underwater thousands of years ago?

Black Sea

Yellow River, China

EUROPE

A S I A

Ur & Kish, Iraq

AFRICA

INDIAN OCEAN

AUSTRALIA

THE DETAILS

ALL THESE ANCIENT flood stories have a few things in common. The floods destroy civilizations, or the whole world, but there's always someone left to start again. In most of the stories, after the flood, a new age begins and the survivors build a better society.

If a worldwide flood really happened, we should be able to see evidence of the changes the water made to the landscape. And sure enough, there are some telltale signs that, long ago, the world did suffer from some seriously soggy disasters.

THE CLUES
Here are just a few of the many clues that point to ancient floods of dramatically deadly proportions.

- **CITY SEDIMENTS** In the 1920s, while exploring the ancient Sumerian cities of Ur and Kish (modern-day Iraq), archaeologists found thick layers of mud underground, with no ancient artifacts buried in them, dating back to about 5,500 years ago. This was flood sediment—mud laid down suddenly by a deluge of dirty water.

- **WRITTEN IN THE ROCKS** In 2007, geologists studying rocks around China's Yellow River also found extra-thick sediment that could only have been left by a big flood. The sediment, almost 4,000 years old, was speckled with green schist, a type of rock only found a long way upstream.

- **BLACK SEA CATASTROPHE** Explorers have found ruins of ancient buildings deep below the Black Sea in Eastern Europe. This evidence suggests that the sea was once much smaller, and the buildings stood on its shores.

THE THEORIES

THERE'S ALSO EVIDENCE for deadly deluges in Australia, India, North America, Africa, and many other places. But they didn't all happen at the same time. So far, there's no proof that one single, supersize flood flowed all over the whole world. Scientists also point out that there isn't actually enough water on our planet to cover all the land at once.

However, there clearly were a lot of floods. Why? Geologists think that in China the Yellow River flood, which probably happened around 4,000 years ago, was caused by a landslide blocking the river and creating a dam. The dam eventually burst,

Vishnu in fish form helps to pull Manu's boat during the flood.

ANCIENT TABLET BEARING THE GILGAMESH FLOOD STORY

releasing a vast amount of water all at once. And in the ancient Sumerian cities of Ur and Kish, flooding was probably common. The area was watered by two huge rivers, which made the land incredibly fertile and good for growing crops, but also put the cities in the flood zone. In other places, floods could have been the result of asteroids and comets. We know these hunks of space rock and ice have hit Earth in the past, sometimes causing tsunamis.

There's another explanation for some of the oldest floods: climate change. We've seen how global warming can cause floods today. When the Earth warmed up after the last ice age ended around 12,000 years ago, this effect was huge. As glaciers and ice caps melted, sea levels rose worldwide. Water could suddenly overflow into a new area, like the Black Sea, or pour out of mountain lakes when natural ice dams melted.

In those days, most people didn't travel far, and no one knew how big the planet really was. If a flood affected a huge area, it probably seemed like the whole world to the people whose cities and lands were destroyed. To those who survived, the event became a powerful story to pass on to future generations.

AN AUSTRALIAN ABORIGINAL MYTH TELLS OF A FROG THAT CAUSED A WORLDWIDE FLOOD.

AN ILLUSTRATION OF ANCIENT GREEK FLOOD SURVIVORS PYRRHA AND DEUCALION

WHY IS THIS MOUNTAIN LAKE FULL OF SKELETONS?

ROOPKUND LAKE

THE BACKGROUND

1 **IN 1942,** a ranger at a nature reserve in the Himalayan mountains in northern India came across a small, frozen lake that seemed to have something very spooky lurking beneath the surface. The ranger leaned in for a closer look and was horrified to see what looked like piles of human bones and skulls trapped in the shallow ice.

There had long been rumors of bones in the remote lake—and it looked as though they were true! The ranger reported his discovery to the authorities. The Second World War was raging, so at first, the government thought that a group of soldiers must have been passing through the area and died of cold.

But when scientists studied the bones, they found they weren't from anyone who had died recently. They were old—really old. And as the ice melted, more and more remains were revealed: the skeletons of dozens and dozens of people. What deadly disaster had happened here?

SKELETON AT LAKE

THE DETAILS

2 **MORE INVESTIGATIONS** revealed that up to 300 people had died at the lake. Some of the bones even had scraps of skin and flesh attached, preserved by the cold. Investigators also found some ancient jewelry, shoes, and spears.

Scientists studied the DNA of the dead, and they found the bones came from two different groups. Some bones belonged to foreigners from far way, while others were from the local area. And weirdly, dating the remains showed that both groups had died at the same time—during the Middle Ages, in the 800s.

THE THEORIES

3 **THE DEATH** of 300 people in one small area certainly signals some kind of serious disaster. People have come up with all kinds of theories about what could have happened. Perhaps it was a landslide or a killer disease epidemic. Or maybe there had been a battle there or a deadly surprise ambush. But nobody could explain what all those people were doing at the remote lake high in the icy mountains in the first place.

NEW EVIDENCE REVEALED!

Local legends and songs from the area tell the story of King Jasdhaval of Kanauj, an ancient kingdom south of the Himalaya. The king went on a pilgrimage to the mountains, taking his family and a huge group of servants, dancers, and musicians. But on their way through the mountains, as they passed the lake, they were caught in a deadly hailstorm, and they all died. This was thought to be no more than a myth.

But in 2013, studies of the skeletons showed how they had died. Almost all had damage to their skulls, caused by something hard and heavy hitting them. Suddenly, the hailstorm story made sense. The injuries matched being struck by giant hailstones between two and three inches (5–8 cm) across. The legend was probably true all along! The visitors may have been King Jasdhaval and his followers, and the locals could have

MYSTERIOUS MONSTERS

Mermaids are just one of many magical creatures found in folklore and fairy tales ... but could they really exist?

DRAGONS, MERMAIDS, GIANTS—they fill story books and imaginations. But turn the clock back a few hundred years, and people believed these creatures really roamed the Earth. Maybe they had good reason. Some people claimed they had seen the bones of real dragons. Some thought they'd spotted mermaids splashing in the seas.

Even today, there are still plenty of reported sightings of cryptids: mysterious monsters or unknown animals. While some people offer up what they call evidence, from photos to hair fibers, so far scientists have never been able to conclusively say that these creatures exist, nor have they been able to capture any of them. So how much of this is rumor or hearsay, and how much is real? Is there evidence that fairytale creatures really walked the Earth?

HALF FISH, HALF HUMAN: FACT OR FICTION?

THE BACKGROUND

IMAGINE YOU'RE ENJOYING a day at the beach, when suddenly, out in the water, you see a real mermaid splashing around and doing a few leaps and dives! Well, that's what happened in Kiryat Yam, Israel, in 2009, according to witnesses. One claimed he'd seen the mermaid lying on the sand before slithering into the water. Many more people described her playing in the sea at sunset, saying she looked like a girl combined with a dolphin. But since that summer, she hasn't been seen again.

Mermaids hit the headlines again in 2012, when a mermaid "documentary" was made for TV. It showed several blurry photos and videos of mermaid-like crea-tures. Unlike fairy-tale mermaids, they were freaky-looking, fast moving, and fierce, and they didn't like being approached by humans. The clips send a shiver down your spine, and they certainly caused a stir—only for the TV company to reveal that the whole thing was made up!

However, that's not the end of this strange sea story. Besides these recent "real-life" sightings, there's a whole ocean's worth of fishy tales of mermaids dating back to ancient times. Are they a myth, or an ongoing marine mystery?

In Scottish legend,
the **BLUE MEN** of the
MINCH are wild mermen,
with blue-gray skin and green beards,
who can cause storms
and sink ships.

A typical mermaid is said
to be a woman with a
fish's tail, but there are
many other types, too.

THE DETAILS

IF YOU BELIEVE the eyewitness accounts, mermaids aren't always the beautiful women with scaly tails found in fairy tales and movies. There are reports of not just female mermaids, but male ones, known as mermen. Some don't even have tails but sport a variety of other features suited to the water, like webbed fingers and toes. Though some reports can be easily explained away, others are curiously convincing.

"MERMAIDS' ROCK," AN 1894 PAINTING BY EDWARD MATTHEW HALE

THE CLUES
If you think you've spotted something that looks like a mermaid, you're in good company. Those who've reported wild mermaid sightings include famous explorers Christopher Columbus and also Henry Hudson, who went on to lend his name to landmarks such as New York's Hudson River.

 NOT CUTE ENOUGH FOR COLUMBUS!
In 1493, during his first voyage to the Americas, Christopher Columbus swore he saw three mermaids near the coast of modern-day Dominican Republic. One of his crew recorded his sighting in the ship's log the next day, but it seems Columbus was less than impressed with the mermaids' looks.

> *On the previous day, when the Admiral went to the Rio del Oro, he saw three mermaids, which rose well out of the sea; but they are not so beautiful as they are painted, though to some extent they have the form of a human face.*

THE MACKEREL MERMAID When sailing north of Norway in 1608, Captain Henry Hudson wrote that two of his crew had seen a mermaid. According to the men, she had white skin, dark hair, and a porpoise-like tail that was "speckled like a mackerel." They had plenty of time to observe her as she swam alongside the ship, staring at the men.

FISH PEOPLE In 1943, during the Second World War, Japanese soldiers were sent to the Kai Islands in Indonesia, where they reported seeing bizarre creatures in the sea. They resembled humans but had pinkish skin, fishy faces with sharp teeth, spikes on their heads, and webbed fingers and toes.

To the soldiers' amazement, the local people agreed that the creatures existed, calling them *orang ikan*, or "fish people."

THE THEORIES

WHAT HAS A ROUND HEAD, a dolphin-like tail, and two "arms"? Besides mermaids, sea mammals called manatees fit this description—and many people think that's what sailors long ago were really seeing when they spotted

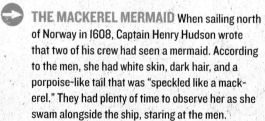

A manatee doesn't look much like modern depictions of mermaids, but some sightings are believed to be these friendly sea mammals.

THE EXPLORER ST. BRENDAN MEETS A MERMAID, IN AN ILLUSTRATION FROM THE 1400S.

"mermaids." This could explain why Christopher Columbus was dismayed that mermaids weren't so glamorous after all!

Manatees move slowly in shallow, tropical water and sometimes appear to "sit" in an upright position. (Though they don't comb their hair with a seashell!) Seafarers could have mistaken them for mermaids, at a distance.

But hang on—what about Henry Hudson? Manatees don't live in the Arctic, where his crew spotted a mermaid. Maybe it was a seal—yet his detailed description doesn't sound much like one.

And as for the mysterious orang ikan, there's still no explanation for the soldiers' spooky story.

Some scientists think that long ago, early humans spent a lot more time in the water than we do now and dove to find food. Could some of them have developed into weird, water-dwelling fish-humans? Probably not, but one thing's for sure: When we discover new species, it's often in the sea—the biggest, least explored habitat on our planet. There are probably plenty of creatures down there that are still unknown to science. Experts think it's highly unlikely that mermaids swim in Earth's oceans, but when you go to the beach, keep a lookout just in case!

• THE CASE •

DRAGONS

ARE FIRE-BREATHING MONSTERS FICTION OR FEARSOME FACT?

THE BACKGROUND

NO TALE OF A BRAVE KNIGHT is complete without a dragon to vanquish. These winged beasts appear in cultures around the world, from the British legends of the ancient King Arthur and his noble knights to the dragon dances that take place each Chinese New Year.

Folktales from China, Korea, and India tell of long snake-like creatures, sometimes with four legs. Legends from Europe describe dragons that can fly and breathe fire, with lizard-like bodies, two or four legs, and leathery wings. In many European tales, dragons are dangerous enemies, while in Chinese mythology, they bring good luck.

But why do so many cultures have dragon legends? They date back centuries, long before the age of instant communications and high-speed travel. That means these stories likely weren't spread by word of mouth—they arose separately in different places. Could it be that long ago, giant fire-breathers actually swarmed the skies?

One of the biggest dragons
in any story is the

JÖRMUNGANDR

of **NORSE MYTH,** which wraps itself
around the whole world.

To most of us, dragons are
instantly recognizable, and
long ago, people believed
they were real.

THE DETAILS

THERE'S PLENTY OF EVIDENCE for dragons lurking in old travel tales, maps, and history books—at least, it looks that way! In the past, many people really believed dragons existed. Some old maps are marked with dragons, perhaps to warn seafarers so they could dodge dragon danger zones. Dragons also turn up in many real-life reports written by explorers and historians. They wrote of creatures similar to lizards or snakes, some with wings and some of enormous size. What could they have been talking about?

A SHIP AND A SEA MONSTER FROM AN OLD MAP

THE CLUES

If you believe ancient writers and mapmakers, you could hardly swing a sword without hitting a dragon in times gone by. History is full of accounts of unnerving run-ins with these menacing monsters. Here are just few examples ...

MARCO POLO'S MONSTERS Famous Italian explorer Marco Polo wrote a book about his travels around Asia in the 1200s. He described many amazing sights, including these creepy snakes with legs:

> *Serpents of such vast size as to strike fear into those who see them ... They have two forelegs ... The head is very big, and the eyes are bigger than loaves of bread. The mouth is large enough to swallow a man whole, and is garnished with great [pointed] teeth ... In the night they go out to feed, and devour every animal they can catch.*

Hmmm ... sounds kind of like a dragon!

HERE BE DRAGONS! The Hunt-Lenox Globe is an old copper globe made in Europe around 1510. It's become infamous for the phrase *Hic sunt dracones*—Latin for "Here be dragons"—written on the globe, close to Southeast Asia.

STRANGE SKELETONS Ancient Greek historian Herodotus wrote about how he went to Arabia to find out more about the "winged serpents" that were said to live there. On arriving, he said, he saw lots of skeletons of the creatures. He described the winged serpents as being "like water-snakes. Their wings are not feathered but very like the wings of a bat."

THE THEORIES

DESCRIPTIONS OF DRAGONS may vary, but they all have one thing in common: Dragons always seem to be described as reptiles. They have scaly skin and long tails, resembling serpents with legs or wings. And they are almost always very big.

A PTEROSAUR FOSSIL

So, are (or were) there any huge, scary reptiles in real life? If you're thinking of dinosaurs, you could be on the right track! One leading theory is that when people long ago found dinosaur fossils, they assumed these huge, lizard-like creatures must still exist. Just like dragon myths, dino fossils are found worldwide. And while dinosaurs didn't have wings, their cousins the pterosaurs did, which could explain why there are winged and nonwinged dragons. Herodotus's "winged serpents" sound like pterosaurs—which would mean the "bones" he saw were actually fossils.

But what about Marco Polo, who described a living dragon-like monster? Well, he may have been a great explorer, but Polo tended to tell some tall tales. His book included several suspicious sightings, such as people with tails and men with dogs' heads. Some think Polo's "dragons" were actually large crocodiles and that his imagination got the best of him.

In fact, several reptiles living today do have some dragon-like features. Crocodiles have massive heads and teeth. Some lizards and snakes can "fly" by gliding from tree to tree. (One gliding lizard is even called the "flying dragon.") Another "dragon," the Komodo dragon, is the world's biggest lizard, reaching 10 feet (3 m) long. And the spitting cobra can shoot burning venom—something a terrified trekker could have misunderstood as fiery "breath." Many of these animals are from Southeast Asia, where dragons were often believed to exist.

However the story of dragons started, it was enough to strike fear into travelers for generations. Now that's a myth with teeth!

The draco lizard or flying dragon is not a real dragon, but one of the closest things alive today—though it's only a few inches long!

33

DID HUMONGOUS HUMANS ONCE WALK THE EARTH?

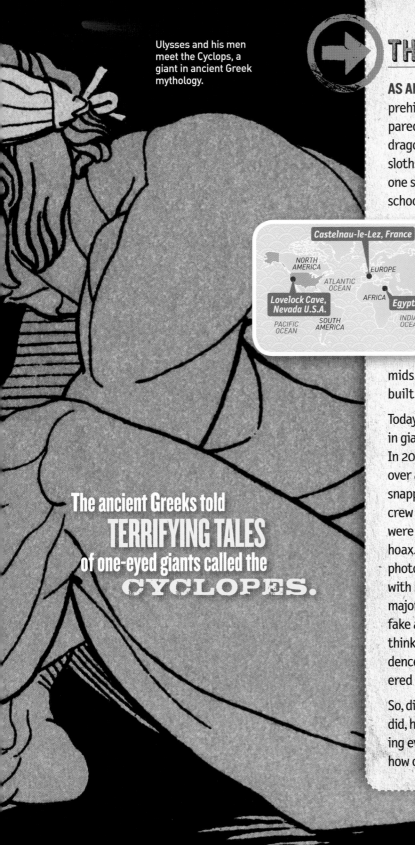

Ulysses and his men meet the Cyclops, a giant in ancient Greek mythology.

The ancient Greeks told
TERRIFYING TALES
of one-eyed giants called the
CYCLOPES.

Castelnau-le-Lez, France

NORTH AMERICA

EUROPE

ATLANTIC OCEAN

AFRICA

Egypt

Lovelock Cave, Nevada U.S.A.

PACIFIC OCEAN

SOUTH AMERICA

INDIAN OCEAN

THE BACKGROUND

AS ANY FOSSIL FAN KNOWS, some prehistoric animals were huge compared to modern versions. There were dragonflies the size of seagulls, giant sloths as big as elephants, and even one supersize shark longer than a school bus!

So it's not so strange to think there could have been giant humans, too. They exist in many fairy tales, myths, and legends. Long ago, when people saw enormous structures like the Egyptian pyramids, they thought giants must have built them.

Today, you might think no one believes in giants anymore, but you'd be wrong! In 2016, a photo of a giant looming over a misty forest, supposedly snapped by a British Royal Air Force crew in 1942, went viral. Many people were convinced—but it was actually a hoax. There are several other "giant" photos too, showing archaeologists with huge skeletons and skulls, but the majority of those have been proven fake as well. Yet a number of believers think there really is convincing evidence for giants—it's just been covered up and kept secret!

So, did giants ever exist, and if they did, how big were they? Some intriguing evidence has been unearthed, but how convincing is it? You decide ...

THE DETAILS

THE TALLEST HUMAN on record, Robert Wadlow, who lived in the United States during the early 20th century, was 8 feet 11 inches (2.72 m) tall. If you met him right now, he'd definitely seem like a giant! But legendary giants are often described as a lot bigger. In Native American stories, the giant Dzunukwa was so big that she could pick whole trees like flowers. In Norse mythology, the giant Skrymir was so vast that humans could walk inside his glove! As for "real-life" giants, reports and relics suggest a range of sizes, from pretty tall to mind-bogglingly enormous.

THE CLUES

Apart from old reports and descriptions, the best evidence for giants comes from a selection of skeletons, skulls, and other body bits.

THE RED-HAIRED GIANTS The Paiute and other Native American peoples have legends about a race of pale-skinned, red-haired giants who lived long ago. They are described as 10 to 12 feet (more than 3 m) tall, and in some cases so tall that ordinary men only came up to their knees. In 1911, miners found human bones in Lovelock Cave in Nevada, U.S.A., where Paiute people said the red-haired giants were buried. Some of these bones were said to be extra-large, but there's not much hard evidence.

THE GIANTS OF CASTELNAU In 1880, anthropologist Georges Vacher de Lapouge explored a Bronze Age burial site in Castelnau-le-Lez, France, and found fragments of huge bones. They were so big that the person they belonged to would have been around 11 feet 6 inches (3.5 m) tall. And in 1894, just a few miles away in Montpellier, the press reported that workers had found giant human skulls. Although pictures of these bones survive, the bones themselves are lost.

THE BIG FINGER In 2012, German newspaper *Bild* reported about a mummified "giant's finger" discovered in Egypt. A local tomb robber had shown the finger to a man named Gregor Spörri,

ROBERT WADLOW

who took several photos of it. He described the 15-inch (38-cm)-long finger's blackened, moldy skin and musty smell. (Eww!) Oddly enough, the tomb robber later vanished, along with his freaky finger, and now the only evidence is the photos.

THE THEORIES

HMM ... these clues sound exciting, but it's hard to be sure when so much of the evidence has mysteriously gone missing! So what's really going on?

Some legendary "giants" could have been based on supertall people, like Robert Wadlow. His height was due to a rare condition that made his pituitary gland, a small organ in the brain, produce too much growth hormone. Other legendary "giants"

AN OLD ILLUSTRATION FROM JACK THE GIANT KILLER, A FAIRY TALE ABOUT A BOY WHO KILLS SEVERAL GIANTS

DAVID AND GOLIATH

could have had the same disorder. In the Bible story of David and Goliath, for example, the giant Goliath is described as nearly 10 feet (3 m) tall. That's not much taller than Wadlow, so it could have been possible. The Castelnau giant was even bigger, perhaps the tallest human ever known.

Could there have once been a whole group of giant humans, like the red-haired giants of the Americas? People from different parts of the world do have different average heights. It's possible that an unusually tall group could have seemed like giants to smaller people, and their height was exaggerated as people passed on stories about them.

But what about really ginormous giants? The owner of the mummified finger would have been taller than 26 feet (8 m), about as tall as a three-story apartment building. Could someone ever be that big? Or was the finger just a freaky (and foul-smelling) fake? Science has the answer to this one: Supermassive humans aren't actually possible. Really big animals are either water dwellers, like the blue whale (as the water supports their weight), or they are four-legged, like the biggest dinosaurs, hippos, and elephants. Humans, on the other hand, have only two legs, and our bones are relatively thin. If a human was scaled up to three-story size, he or she would be four times taller than normal but 64 times heavier. The bones of someone this size would be unable to support that kind of weight. So there may have been a few "giants" in the past—but not very big ones!

WHERE IS MONGOLIA'S MYSTERIOUS MONSTER HIDING?

AN ARTIST'S DEPICTION OF WHAT
A DEATH WORM LOOKS LIKE

A MONSTER
movie inspired by the
MONGOLIAN DEATH WORM
was made in 2010—
with death worms
the size of elephants.

THE BACKGROUND

IF YOU EVER GO TREKKING in Mongolia's Gobi desert, beware of the deadly Death Worm that's said to lurk beneath the desert sand. If you do stumble over it, it could squirt killer acid at you, turning your skin yellow before you collapse in agony. Or, if that doesn't work, it might zap you to death with a powerful electric shock strong enough to fell a camel.

At least that's what the locals may tell you. They call this bad-tempered beast the *olgoi-khorkhoi*, meaning "large intestine worm." That's because it's said to be dark red and as thick as your arm, like a piece of large intestine. Yuck! To the rest of the world, though, it's known as the Mongolian Death Worm.

But is it a real animal? Many Mongolians say it is, and they can describe it in detail. It seems everyone has a friend or relative who's seen the Death Worm. Since outsiders first heard these stories in the early 1900s, the mystery has become an obsession. Zoologists, explorers, and TV crews have set out to search for the Death Worm. But so far, it remains a cryptid—a creatures we can't prove really exists.

The Gobi, home to the well-known but rarely sighted Mongolian Death Worm

THE DETAILS

IF YOU WANT TO SPOT the Mongolian Death Worm, here's what to look out for: It's described as two to three feet (0.6–1 m) long, thick, smooth, squishy, and dark red, with spikes on one or possibly both ends. It usually burrows under the ground, leaving a ripple on the surface. And it likes to hang out near the saxaul plant, which has yellow flowers. In fact, it's said to like the color yellow and can be attracted to yellow objects such as toys or clothes. Sometimes, after a rare desert rainfall, it may come to the surface and poke its horrifying head out of the sand.

THE CLUES

The best clues we have that the Death Worm exists are a series of eyewitness accounts. Are these convincing, questionable, or total baloney ... what do you think?

 ANDREWS' ADVENTURE In 1922, naturalist and explorer Roy Chapman Andrews went to Mongolia to search for fossils. When he asked government officials for permission, Mongolia's prime minister gave him an extra task—to look for the olgoi-khorkhoi and catch one if possible! The prime minister described it as sausage-shaped, two feet (0.6 m) long, and deadly if touched. Andrews promised to use a pair of tongs to grab one—but sadly never managed to spot the worm.

SUGI'S STORY Czech cryptid-hunter Ivan Mackerle went in search of the Death Worm in 1990. Like Andrews, he failed to find the giant worm, but he did collect lots of information from locals. His interpreter, a man named Sugi, told Mackerle about some scientists who had once visited his home village in the Gobi. One of them was using a metal rod to dig in the sand when he suddenly collapsed and died. When the others ran toward him, they saw a huge red worm emerging from the ground.

FREEMAN'S FINDINGS Another cryptid-hunter, Richard Freeman, joined an expedition to Mongolia in 2005. He recorded many eyewitness accounts of the Death Worm. People told him how they had run away after seeing the worm, or how it had killed people by spitting at them. One man named Damdin described seeing a Death Worm when he was young. He told his parents, who were so scared that they moved the family to a new area!

THE THEORIES

SO, WHAT'S THE VERDICT? Despite the lack of hard evidence, visitors to Mongolia are often impressed by local accounts and believe there really is something out there—though it might not be quite as exciting as the bloodcurdlingly vicious Death Worm.

If there is an undiscovered animal in the Gobi, experts say it's probably a reptile, not a worm. Worms prefer damp habitats and would soon dry out in the desert sand. Instead, maybe the mysterious "worm" is an unknown snake. Some snakes spit venom, and some can burrow in sand, like the sand boa. Or perhaps it's an amphisbaenian, or "worm lizard"—a burrowing, legless reptile with a large head. Their smooth scales are arranged in rings, which makes them resemble worms. It's also true that some animals can generate electricity, like the electric eel. So it's possible that there could be an animal out there that looks and acts like the Death Worm. The Gobi is huge, and the worm seems to be good at hiding. So maybe we just haven't found it yet.

On the other hand, it's kind of suspicious that despite the many efforts to track it down, no one has managed to snap a photo of a Mongolian Death Worm. No dead specimens, skeletons, or fossils have ever been found. As cryptids go, this one is not very convincing.

Even so, if you do see a strange wormlike beast in the Gobi, don't poke it. And avoid wearing yellow—just in case!

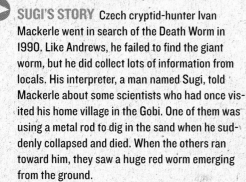

SAXAUL PLANT

IVAN MACKERLE

AN ARTIST'S DEPICTION OF
THE LEGENDARY DEATH WORM

MOVE OVER NESSIE.
MEET
CHAMP!

THE BACKGROUND

LOCH NESS in Scotland is famous for the Loch Ness Monster, or "Nessie," but did you know that many other lakes around the world have monsters, too? One of the most frequently spotted and studied is "Champ," the Lake Champlain Monster.

Lake Champlain is a long, deep lake in North America, divided between the United States and Canada. For centuries, people living nearby have reported monster sightings. The area's early inhabitants, the Iroquois and Abenaki peoples, believed a huge, horned serpent lived in the lake and warned explorers not to disturb it. In 1819, a man named Captain Crum described seeing a giant, fast-moving water monster with a seahorse-like head. In 1873, the monster appeared to railway workers, who saw bright, flashing scales and a wide, toothy mouth. The same year, it bumped into a boatful of tourists, who said it squirted water into the air and glittered in the sun as it zoomed away. American showman P.T. Barnum was so convinced he offered a reward of $50,000 to anyone who could bring him the hide of the serpent.

As the reports spread, more people came forward to share their similar stories, and there are now more than 300 sightings on record. But is the monster really there?

CANADA

UNITED STATES

QUEBEC (CANADA)

MAINE

Lake Champlain

VERMONT

NEW YORK

NEW HAMPSHIRE

Peaceful, beautiful Lake Champlain, where a monster is said to roam

In case it does exist, the states of Vermont and New York have passed laws **PROTECTING** the Lake Champlain MONSTER from being hunted or harmed.

THE DETAILS

MOST DESCRIPTIONS of Champ seem to be creepily consistent, suggesting the same animal has been spotted again and again over the centuries. Witnesses often report a seahorse-like head and water-spraying nostrils. The head is on a long, snaky neck, often seen sticking up above the surface. The creature's body is long and serpentine, and it is sometimes seen as a series of humps that appear above the surface as the animal moves through the water. And this critter is big: It's usually reported as between 20 feet and 80 feet (6–24 m) long, or sometimes even bigger.

THE CLUES

Some of the most exciting and eerie evidence is also the most recent, thanks to modern technology. In the past 50 years, the monster— or something monstrous-looking, at least—has been caught on camera, in both a famous still shot and in a spooky video. There are even sound recordings that might reveal there's something strange lurking in the lake ...

THE MYSTERIOUS MANSI PHOTO In the summer of 1977, Sandra Mansi stopped by the lake during a road trip with her family. As her children played near the shore, she was amazed to see something rise out of the water in the distance—first a head, then a neck and a humped body. She managed to take one photograph, the now famous "Mansi photo."

THE FREAKY FISHING BOAT VIDEO In 2005, two men fishing on Lake Champlain saw something weird moving in the water alongside their boat and managed to catch it on video. Though whatever it is stays underwater, the video shows shapes that look like a flipper, a long neck, and a narrow head with a visible mouth. The men said it was unlike any animal they had ever seen.

UNDERWATER SOUNDS Twice, in 2003 and 2014, investigators recorded unexplained noises in the lake. They sound similar to the clicking noises that whales and dolphins make when they use echolocation to find prey. But whales and dolphins don't live in Lake Champlain.

THE THEORIES

IS IT A FISH? Is it a prehistoric sea creature long thought extinct? Or is it just a floating log? What could Champ really be?

As with the Loch Ness Monster, reports often mention a long neck and a humpback. This sounds very much like a plesiosaur, an ancient water reptile that lived around the same time as

THE MANSI PHOTO

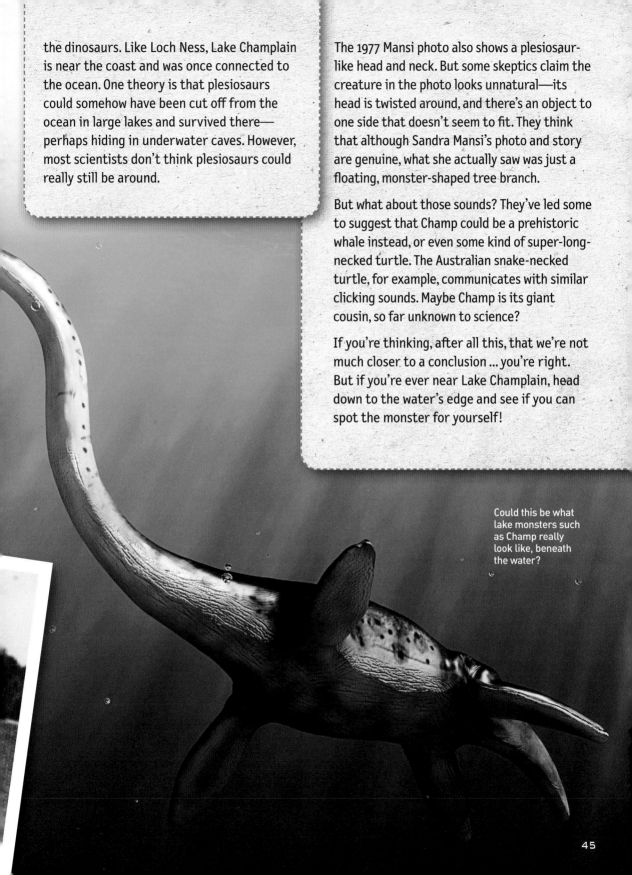

the dinosaurs. Like Loch Ness, Lake Champlain is near the coast and was once connected to the ocean. One theory is that plesiosaurs could somehow have been cut off from the ocean in large lakes and survived there—perhaps hiding in underwater caves. However, most scientists don't think plesiosaurs could really still be around.

The 1977 Mansi photo also shows a plesiosaur-like head and neck. But some skeptics claim the creature in the photo looks unnatural—its head is twisted around, and there's an object to one side that doesn't seem to fit. They think that although Sandra Mansi's photo and story are genuine, what she actually saw was just a floating, monster-shaped tree branch.

But what about those sounds? They've led some to suggest that Champ could be a prehistoric whale instead, or even some kind of super-long-necked turtle. The Australian snake-necked turtle, for example, communicates with similar clicking sounds. Maybe Champ is its giant cousin, so far unknown to science?

If you're thinking, after all this, that we're not much closer to a conclusion ... you're right. But if you're ever near Lake Champlain, head down to the water's edge and see if you can spot the monster for yourself!

Could this be what lake monsters such as Champ really look like, beneath the water?

COULD THE **CURIOUSLY CREEPY KAPPA REALLY** EXIST?

THE BACKGROUND

IF YOU EVER VISIT JAPAN, take care near rivers and ponds—especially if you see a DANGER sign by the water with a picture of a small, green human-shaped creature on it. This is the mysterious, mythical water monster known as the kappa.

The name *kappa* means "river child," and kappa are said to be child-size, with green or yellow scaly skin, webbed hands and feet, and beaklike mouths. Kappa are incredibly strong and can be deadly. They may grab people, or even horses, and drown them. They're used as a cautionary tale to warn children not to play near water, as they're said to sneak up on kids, drag them underwater, and eat them. Don't say we didn't warn you!

The kappa's freakiest feature is a bowl-shaped dent on its head, filled with water. When the kappa leaves its lake or river and ventures onto dry land, this water provides its life force—but the kappa has to be careful not to spill it. One way to outsmart a kappa is to bow to it. Despite their horrible habits, kappa are famously polite—so it will bow back, spill its water, and lose its life force! Another way is to throw cucumbers (a kappa's favorite food) into the water to keep it happy.

ASIA

JAPAN

RUSSIA

NORTH KOREA

SOUTH KOREA

Sea of Japan

JAPAN

PACIFIC OCEAN

The kappa maki
is a type of
JAPANESE SUSHI ROLL
made with cucumber—
the perfect food for the
KAPPA.

Kappabuchi in northern
Japan is still said to be
home to the kappa.

このへんは
こわいぞ

独立行政法人 水資源機構
見沼土地改良区

A KAPPA SIGN IN JAPAN

THE DETAILS

YOU MIGHT THINK all this sounds like nothing more than silly, harmless folklore and fairy tales, but many people in Japan used to be genuinely scared of kappa, and some still are. There are parts of the country where kappa are said to lurk to this day. And there's also some eerie evidence that some think shows they really do exist, or at least they did in times gone by.

THE CLUES
On the trail of the real-life kappa? Check out these creepy clues from the past ...

SPOOKY SIGHTINGS There are detailed historical reports of kappa being seen, and even caught in fishing nets, in the 1700s and 1800s. More recently, two Japanese policemen spotted a kappa-like creature beside a road in the 1970s. In 1984, a fisherman reported seeing a group of kappa leap into a river, leaving strange footprints behind.

KNOW YOUR KAPPA! In the Edo period of Japanese history, between 1603 and 1867, people actually studied kappa as a serious subject. There's even a kappa guidebook from 1820, called the *Suikokouryaku*, full of helpful information and pictures.

KAPPA CURIOSITIES Several temples and museums claim to have mummified kappa, or kappa body parts. They include an arm and foot said to be from a kappa from the year 1818.

A KAPPA LEAVES THE WATER IN AN OLD JAPANESE ILLUSTRATION.

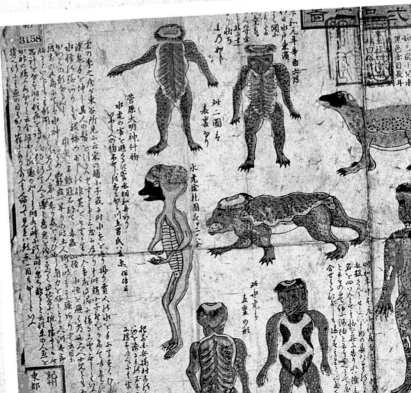

A guide to different types of kappa in a Japanese kappa encyclopedia called the *Suikokouryaku*, dating from 1820

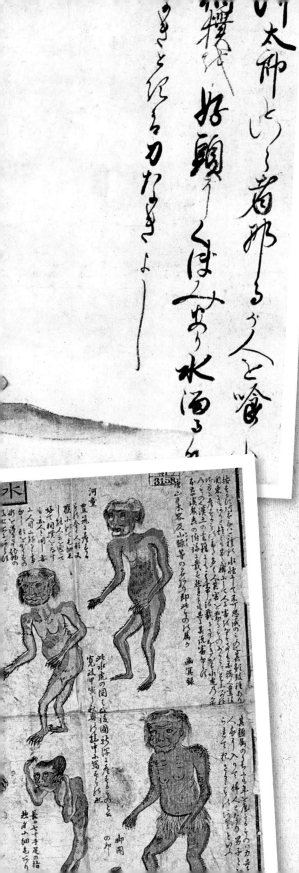

THE THEORIES

IS, OR WAS, THE KAPPA REAL? Or is it just a made-up bogeyman? As with some other cryptids, there are theories that other, more normal animals have been mistaken for kappa—such as turtles or Japanese macaques, which are monkeys that often sit in rivers. The Japanese giant salamander grows to the size of a large child and can bite, while the river otter has a humanlike face and can stand up on its hind legs. Combine a distant sighting of one of these creatures with stories of water-dwelling humanoids and you could end up with a "kappa" sighting.

Or could the kappa be an actual river creature unknown to modern science? With their small size, beaks, and webbed hands and feet, kappa are strangely similar to the orang ikan, the fish-human reported in the 1940s (see page 28). Could the kappa be its river relative?

As for those macabre mummies, some of them appear to be fakes made from fused-together parts of monkeys, fish, and other animals. But other remains, like the arm and foot, are more mysterious. They don't look like any known animal, and they're spookily kappa-like.

Even if they are out there, kappa sightings seem to be getting rarer these days. So there's probably nothing to worry about. But don't forget your cucumbers, just in case.

JAPANESE GIANT SALAMANDER

ARE MINIATURE HUMANS ALIVE & WELL IN INDONESIA'S JUNGLES?

THE BACKGROUND

1 **THE ISLAND OF SUMATRA,** Indonesia is home to some of the world's rarest and most elusive animals, such as the orangutan and the Sumatran tiger. And if you believe the locals, something else lives there, too— a creature that has been reported and described many times, but that no one has yet managed to prove exists. Called the *orang pendek,*

ORANG PENDEK DEPICTION

meaning "short person," it's around three or four feet (1 m) tall, walks on two legs, and has a humanlike face. Though small, it's strong, and it sometimes raids crops or breaks into human homes to steal food. To stay on the orang pendek's good side, some people even leave gifts at the edge of the forest.

It's not only locals who claim to have spotted this strange species. Dutch settlers in the early 1900s reported seeing strange creatures that were not men or orangutans, but something in between.

THE DETAILS

2 **BIOLOGISTS** and cryptozoologists, intrigued by the reports, have spent years on the trail of the orang pendek. They've

collected dozens of descriptions and cataloged evidence such as footprints, chewed food, and even samples of the creature's hair. One British researcher, Debbie Martyr, reported actually seeing an orang pendek herself as it strolled across a valley. There are even some blurry photos and videos that claim to show the creature, but it's hard to tell if they are genuine.

THE THEORIES

3 **MOST SCIENTISTS AGREE** that the orang pendek, if it exists, seems to be a member of the ape family. The footprints and facial features people describe sound ape-like, and testing of hair said to be from an orang pendek also showed it was from an ape. But what kind of ape—a new species or an existing one? There are multiple theories. Some say that "witnesses" are in fact seeing other animals, like orangutans, monkeys, or even children. Others think the orang pendek is just folklore.

But many people disagree. Several cryptid-hunters are sure it does exist and that it will soon be found. Some think it's an unknown forest ape, related to the orangutan. But others say it could be more closely related to humans.

NEW EVIDENCE REVEALED!

IN 2003, the science world was stunned by an amazing discovery on another Indonesian island, Flores. Inside a cave, archaeologists found ancient human bones. But they were unlike any ever seen before: These bones belonged to tiny people, only around three feet (1 m) tall! Scientists named them *Homo floresiensis*, though they are also nicknamed "hobbits." Previously unknown to science, they were a species of early human that became extinct about 50,000 years ago, perhaps when a volcano exploded on their island.

But what if they didn't all die in the disaster? Could some of those hobbit-humans have survived in the forests and evolved into the orang pendek? Scientists don't think this is likely, but that hasn't stopped some people from trekking through the jungle in search of this lost human species.

3

UNDERWATER
MYSTERIES

SINCE HUMANS can't breathe underwater, we don't spend a lot of time there—and that means that plenty of submerged mysteries from history have gone undiscovered for thousands of years. Sometimes it's only recent technology, like sonar and scuba gear, that has allowed these watery wonders to finally surface.

Over the past 11,000 years or so, the Earth has warmed, ice has melted, and water levels have risen. So today's seas and lakes cover many areas that used to be land—land where people lived, hunted, and built things long ago. Some discoveries could point to ancient civilizations that were once known only as legends. But it's so difficult to study ruins and remains that are drowned under deep water that in many cases, the jury is still out. So come on, climb into your diving gear, and let's take a closer look at the mysteries beneath the waves.

A scuba diver in the
Sea of Japan

NATURAL ROCK FORMATION

OR STRANGE ANCIENT STRUCTURE?

Divers explore one of the
remarkably flat, square-edged
platforms on the Yonaguni
Monument.

Every year from November to May, thousands of **HAMMERHEAD SHARKS** swim past the island of **YONAGUNI** as part of their winter migration.

ASIA
JAPAN

CHINA
NORTH KOREA
SOUTH KOREA
JAPAN
East China Sea
PACIFIC OCEAN
Yonaguni Island

THE BACKGROUND

AROUND 1987, Japanese diver Kihachiro Aratake was exploring the sea near the island of Yonaguni, looking for good places to spot hammerhead sharks. As he swam, he realized he was surrounded by something weird—what looked like artificial platforms, walls, and steps. After Aratake reported what he had seen, a marine geologist, Masaaki Kimura, began to investigate. Not far below the water's surface, he found a huge structure that seemed to be carved with steps, paths, geometric shapes, and even unknown writing or symbols.

Kimura studied and mapped the site for the next 20 years. He became convinced that ancient people had deliberately shaped the structure, now known as the Yonaguni Monument. It could even be the remains of a lost city or civilization now sunk beneath the waves.

But for this to be true, the Yonaguni Monument must have been made when this part of the seabed was above water. That would mean at least 10,000 years ago, when sea levels were much lower. Unless, that is, it was built more recently, on land that then sank into the sea, thanks to an earthquake. Could Kimura be right—did ancient people create this enormous geometric puzzle? Or, as some scientists think, is this "monument" really just the natural work of the waves?

THE DETAILS

IN TOTAL, the mysterious monument measures almost 500 feet (150 m) long and 130 feet (40 m) wide. It's 90 feet (27 m) high, with the top only 16 feet (5 m) below the water's surface, and it is made of sandstone rock. Its puzzling features include a wide ledge running around the base, several sets of steps, and large, flat platforms on different levels. Unlike most ancient pyramids and other monuments, Yonaguni is not symmetrical—in fact, it's kind of a mixed-up muddle. Yet many parts do look deliberately designed.

THE CLUES

The monument has many matching regular shapes and angles, as well as peculiar parts that look as if they have some kind of important purpose. Could they all have appeared by accident?

SUPERSIZE STEPS The steps up the sides often make people think the monument must be human-made, since they look so regular and deliberate. But there's a problem: Most of them are massive! Unless the makers themselves were giants, they couldn't have walked up them. So what were they for?

TRIANGLES, TURTLES, AND HOLES The monument also has many other features that don't look natural. They include a feature known as "the turtle," because it resembles the animal; a pool or basin with a row of round holes along the edge; and several neat triangle and right-angled shapes.

WRITING ON THE WALL? Kimura has discovered peculiar patterns carved into the rocks of the monument. Are they natural scratch marks, pictures of animals, or perhaps a type of ancient, unknown writing?

THE THEORIES

WHEN PEOPLE SEE the Yonaguni Monument, whether in pictures or in real life on a dive, they're often completely convinced that it's the work of humans. All those steps, shapes, and platforms just look too perfect to have appeared on their own!

But ask other geologists who've been to check it out, and they'll tell a different story. They think it really could be natural, thanks to the way sandstone rock forms. Sandstone builds up in smooth, flat layers and has natural cracks that grow in straight lines. The monument's location close to the coast puts it in the perfect spot for waves to break off pieces along those lines, leaving neat shapes behind. The earthquakes common in Japan could have played a part, too. And the "carvings" could be scratches made by pebbles or animals.

STEP FORMATION

Scuba divers explore the turtle feature on the monument.

It might seem odd, but it's common for rock to have regular shapes. Some types of volcanic rock can form into hexagons as they cool, for example. And some of the cliffs on land near the Yonaguni Monument also have natural step shapes in them.

But wait a minute! Those who side with Masaaki Kimura point out it's still unlikely that all those shapes would have appeared so close together—and some features, like the rows of holes, are pretty hard to explain.

If humans did make the monument, what was it for? Maybe it was a base for now vanished buildings or a ceremonial site for holding religious rituals or sacrifices, like the Aztec pyramids. Some say it looks like a boat dock. The steps on the sides could have been landing jetties, linked together by wooden steps or ladders.

So far, the two sides can't agree, but some have suggested a compromise: The monument could be a mostly natural site to which people added shapes and carvings. Even if that's true, we still don't know who these people were or when they lived. This is one mystery that's still waiting to be solved.

IS THE UNDERWATER CAVERN CURSED?

A SKULL RESTS AT THE BOTTOM OF A CENOTE ONCE USED FOR HUMAN SACRIFICES.

Many Mexican **CENOTES** are connected by a vast network of **WATER-FILLED** underground tunnels, stretching at least 215 miles (346 km).

THE BACKGROUND

EXPLORING UNDERGROUND caves is exciting, but it's also difficult, dark, and dangerous. Now imagine trekking through caverns that are not just pitch black and spooky, but also full of water! You need scuba gear and an oxygen supply, and if you get lost or stuck, you're in serious trouble. But for explorers who want to learn more about our world, this high-risk activity, called cave diving, is a way to discover information about our past ... and sometimes to uncover the truth behind ancient mysteries.

A cenote is a sinkhole that forms when fragile limestone bedrock collapses. These jungle sinkholes then flood with groundwater to become deep pools. They're common in Mexico, which has thousands of them. Cenotes were important to Mexico's Maya people, who believed they were gateways to the underworld or the homes of the gods. Some cenotes were also a source of freshwater for Maya cities.

But rumor has it that one creepy cenote contains more than just water—it's cursed! Sac Uayum, located near the 800-year-old ruins of the Maya city of Mayapán, is said to be guarded by a feathered serpent with a horse's head that will snatch anyone who ventures too close. This curse lives on—today's local people don't go near the cenote. In 2013, when cave explorers decided to explore Sac Uayum, local villagers performed a traditional ceremony before the dive to ask the dangerous demon for permission to enter.

And when the explorers finally dove down into the notoriously haunted cavern, they did find something spooky: The cenote contained at least 17 human skulls as well as a jumble of other bones!

NORTH AMERICA

MEXICO

PACIFIC OCEAN

Gulf of Mexico

Sac Uayum

Caribbean Sea

MEXICO

BELIZE

GUATEMALA

HONDURAS

PACIFIC OCEAN

EL SALVADOR

THE DETAILS

DURING THE DIVE, explorers found an opening at the bottom of the cenote. It led to another huge water-filled chamber. This cave was dark and enclosed, with no opening to the surface—yet there were skeletons in there, too.

These discoveries raised lots of questions. Who did the skeletons belong to, and why were they put there? And how did anyone get them into the second, hidden chamber, long before the days of scuba diving?

THE CLUES

There must be a reason that people have long feared this cenote. And there must be an explanation for how those bones got there. These clues might hold the answers ...

FLAT HEADS Many of the skulls in the cenote had a strange shape: They were flattened at the front and back. What had happened to them?

UNDER THE RUBBLE A lot of the bones were found half-buried in piles of broken stones. Why?

THE CURVING CITY WALL Mayapán, the ruined Maya city near the Sac Uayum cenote, was surrounded by a city wall. This wall seems to curve inward to avoid the cenote, making sure it was left outside the city. But other nearby cenotes were left inside the walls, probably to provide drinking water.

LONG-LOST BONES

The dark depths of the cenote, captured on camera by divers

THE THEORIES

YOU MIGHT BE THINKING that the people who ended up at the bottom of Sac Uayum simply fell in by accident. After all, a deep, steep-sided, water-filled hole could easily claim a few lives. However, archaeologists have other ideas.

The flattened skulls show the skeletons were probably Maya people. There was nothing wrong with them: They'd had their heads squashed deliberately! The Maya, like several other ancient cultures, used boards to shape young children's skulls while they were still soft. Experts think they may have seen flat heads as noble and godlike.

Another Mexican cenote, Cenote Sagrado, or Sacred Cenote, also contains skeletons. These bones show signs of injury, so archaeologists think people were sacrificed to the gods then were flung into the water. But the Sac Uayum skeletons don't have these marks.

As the Maya believed cenotes were connected to the underworld, is it possible they simply used the cenote as a place to bury their dead? This seems unlikely, because the Maya normally buried people in the ground and close to their homes.

There's one last theory that might make sense. This cenote could have been chosen as a place to put people who had died from diseases, to keep them away from the city and prevent infection from spreading to healthy inhabitants. That could explain why the Maya kept the cenote outside the city wall and didn't drink its water. The legend of the serpent helped to keep people safely away.

As for the cenote's second chamber, the explorers realized that a wall of rock between the two chambers looked as if it had collapsed, long after the bodies had been put there. Some of the bones fell through into the second chamber, along with piles of rubble.

There may be more to discover in the cenote, and more bones to uncover ... as long as the feathered serpent is happy to let the divers return, that is!

A diver examines Maya remains in Sac Uayam.

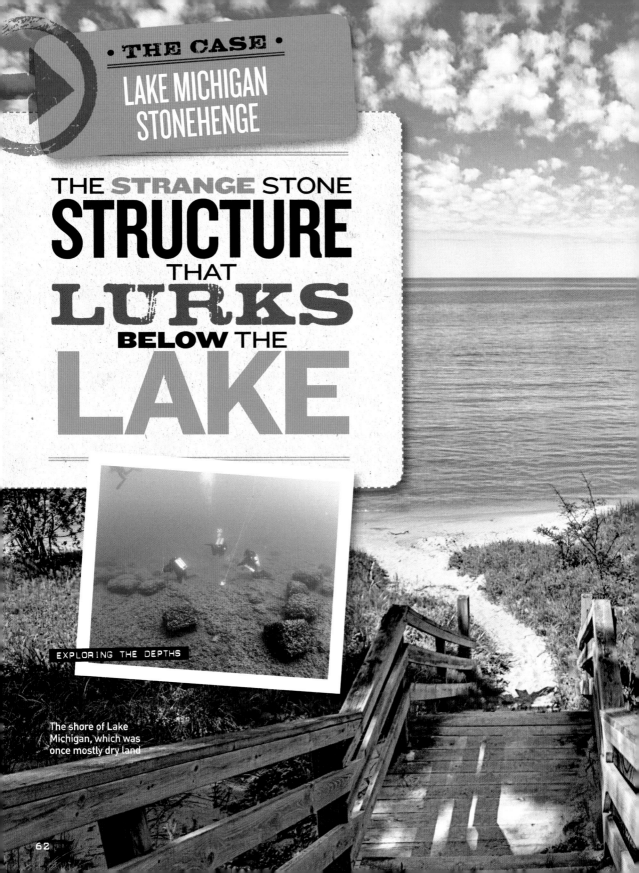

THE **STRANGE** STONE
STRUCTURE
THAT
LURKS
BELOW THE
LAKE

EXPLORING THE DEPTHS

The shore of Lake Michigan, which was once mostly dry land

THE BACKGROUND

IN 2007, archaeologists were scanning the bottom of the United States' Lake Michigan with sonar equipment to look for old shipwrecks. But the explorers found something much stranger: Beneath the surface they discovered a collection of stones on the lake bed. However, instead of a natural-looking pile, the rocks looked as if they were carefully chosen and arranged in a pattern. The team decided to send divers to see if the sonar readings weren't just a mistake.

When divers went down to investigate, they found that the stones did indeed look like they had been arranged deliberately. Some are even in roughly circular patterns, while others form a long line. Even more exciting, one of the stones seemed to have a carving on it. It looked like a mastodon, a prehistoric elephant-like animal. Could this be the work of ancient people who lived in the area eons ago?

When news of the discovery broke, it became known on the internet as the "Lake Michigan Stonehenge", a reference to the famous prehistoric world heritage site in England. But the rocks on the lake bottom aren't really much like England's Stonehenge, which has bigger, squarer stones.

And the newly discovered underwater architecture isn't actually a "henge" (defined as a circular mound) at all. And what about the mastodon "carving"—did the stone's natural cracks and grooves just happen to resemble the animal?

Experts have yet to crack the case, and they are planning on studying the site further. But for now, whether this lake location is human-made or just a natural coincidence is still shrouded in mystery.

A MASTODON was similar to a woolly mammoth, but slightly smaller, with shorter TUSKS and a less bumpy head.

THE DETAILS

THE DISCOVERY is in a part of the lake named Grand Traverse Bay. It lies under 40 feet (12 m) of water, and the line of stones that makes up part of the formation is around a mile (1.6 km) long. It definitely seems to have been built by humans, but when—and what was it for? Is it really an ancient monument, like the more famous Stonehenge? And how did it end up at the bottom of a lake?

THE CLUES Lake Michigan is a seriously long way from Stonehenge, and it's unlikely that the two sites are connected. But there are other clues closer to home that could explain more.

ABOVE: A section of one of the lines of stones

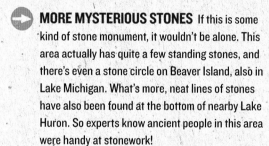 **MORE MYSTERIOUS STONES** If this is some kind of stone monument, it wouldn't be alone. This area actually has quite a few standing stones, and there's even a stone circle on Beaver Island, also in Lake Michigan. What's more, neat lines of stones have also been found at the bottom of nearby Lake Huron. So experts know ancient people in this area were handy at stonework!

FLOODED FORESTS At the other end of Lake Michigan, near the city of Chicago, Illinois, scientists have found the stumps of ancient oak, ash, and hickory trees on the lake bed, in water 80 feet (24 m) deep. This means that some parts of Lake Michigan were once dry land.

END OF MASTODONS Did mastodons live here? Fossils show that they did: In fact, they were common just south of Lake Michigan. However, the age of the fossils also indicates that mastodons died out here at least 9,000 years ago.

THE THEORIES

THOUGH IT MAY NOT BE the most perfect pattern in the world, the stones of Lake Michigan do look as if they were put there on purpose.

Since we know ancient people in the area had a habit of doing this, this theory could hold water—especially if experts discover that the "mastodon" on one of the stones is a human carving.

The ancient underwater trees in Lake Michigan have been dated to 8,000 years ago, when glaciers were melting after the last ice age and the water level was much lower. People could have lived on land that is now a lake bed. And they may have hunted mastodons. Early people often made images of prey animals, which could explain the carving. But if the stone structure was made when the lake bed was dry and there were mastodons around, it's at least 9,000 years

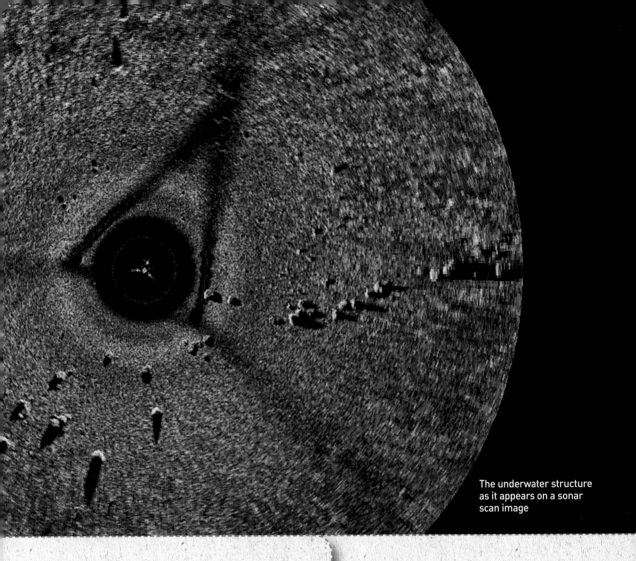

The underwater structure as it appears on a sonar scan image

old! There aren't many ancient stone monuments that old—although some do exist, such as Göbekli Tepe (see page 102).

Could the stones be a ceremonial site, or were they a calendar for tracking the sun's movements, like Stonehenge? It's hard to tell, but some people think they could be linked to the spooky Lake Michigan Triangle—the Great Lakes' version of the Bermuda Triangle. These people say the stones have some kind of ancient energy that could explain why several boats and planes have gone missing while crossing Lake Michigan. (Scientists say maybe it's just the strong winds.)

Or perhaps the truth is a little more practical. The stones at the bottom of nearby Lake Huron are arranged in two long lines. Experts say this is probably a drive line, used to funnel prey animals in one direction so hunters could trap and catch them more easily. The Lake Michigan stones also form a long line. Maybe they were part of an ancient mastodon trap!

Without more studies, it's hard to tell. But the archaeologists are planning to go back, and they're hoping to find more evidence. They might just surface with the truth!

A SUNKEN UFO ON THE SEABED ... OR NOT?

AN ILLUSTRATION OF THE ANOMALY

flying saucer that had sunk to the bottom of the sea. That would be proof, right?

In 2011, a team of shipwreck hunters was scanning the Baltic Sea in northern Europe with sonar, searching for old sunken ships that could contain treasure. Near the uninhabited island of Gotska Sandön, their equipment revealed an unusual, almost circular object on the flat seabed. Though the image wasn't super clear, its shape immediately reminded people of spaceships from sci-fi movies, such as the well-known *Millennium Falcon* from *Star Wars*—sparking a thrilling theory that the object was a crashed UFO. It was named the "Baltic Sea anomaly," meaning something unusual and out of place.

THE BACKGROUND

1 **DO ALIENS EXIST?** There are plenty of people who say they've seen flying saucers visiting our planet. But it's hard to prove any of these sightings. So imagine if we found a crashed

THE DETAILS

2 **THE STRANGE STRUCTURE** appeared to be about 200 feet (60 m) across and had features on its surface that resembled straight ridges and steps. The sonar even seemed to show a "track" leading up to the object, as if it had skidded to a halt. Obviously, this called for further investigation. But when the team returned to the same spot to try to capture better images, they reported that most of their electrical equipment mysteriously stopped working!

THE THEORIES

3 **OF COURSE,** when the story made the headlines, UFO fans had a field day! Many were sure this must be a real spacecraft from an alien fleet, resting in a watery grave after an epic battle or some kind of high-tech engine failure. Artists' impressions of the object circulated on the internet, and fueled theories that it might be a flying saucer.

Other people raised the possibility it could be a secret anti-submarine base, or part of an ancient city now covered by the sea—maybe even the legendary lost city of Atlantis.

But geologists and other scientists weren't so sure, pointing out that the anomaly could just as easily be an unusually round rock. Only an expert investigation could reveal the truth.

THE STAR WARS MILLENNIUM FALCON

NEW EVIDENCE REVEALED!

IN 2012, divers managed to locate the mysterious mass on the seabed and collect samples from it. When scientists looked at those samples, they reported they were made of stone—not metal nor any unknown alien spaceship-building material. These experts say the most likely explanation is that the anomaly is an extra-large lump of rock, transported to its location by the glaciers that flowed through this area during the last

where the glacier pushed it along. Did that put the alien spaceship theories to rest? Errr ... no. After all, as UFO fans claim, if aliens have gravity-defying technology, there would be nothing to stop them from building a spaceship from stone anyway. Or perhaps, they say, this UFO is so old that it's become fossilized. Well, we'll believe that when the rest of the alien fleet turns up!

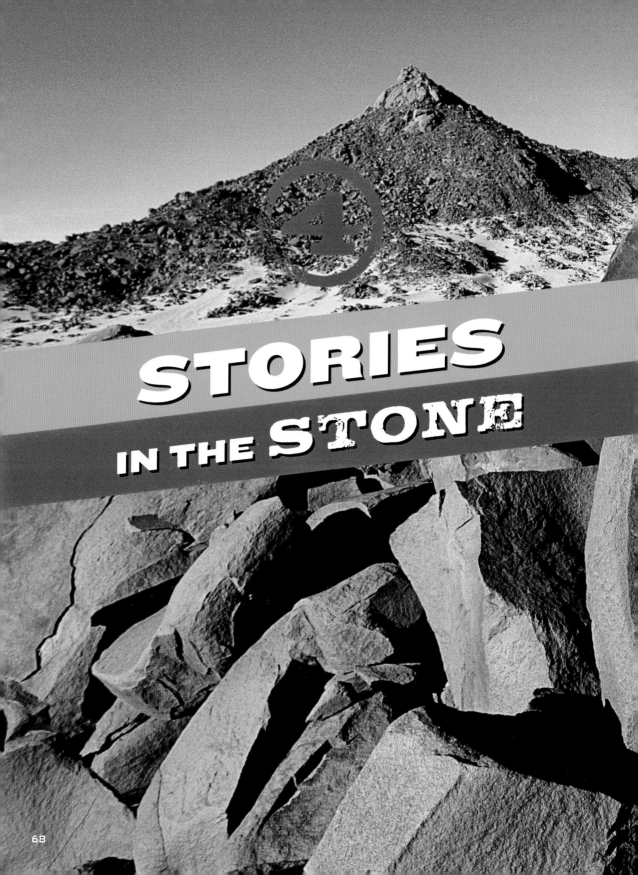

STORIES
IN THE STONE

Rock art in Niger, Africa, dating from around 1000 B.C., shows two figures who are thought to be warriors.

PEOPLE FROM THE PAST have left their mark on stones all over the world, whether as ancient inscriptions and symbols, cave paintings, or strange rock structures. And there are many more marks and patterns that may or may not be human-made.

The mysterious messages in this chapter could come from many sources. Some seem magical, but they might have been written in the rocks by nature itself. Others could contain clues about Stone Age societies and prehistoric peoples. And some are said to reveal the truth about alien landings, or even time-traveling visitors from the future. All this from some old carvings and stone shapes? Turn the page to see if you can crack some of these rocky riddles.

WHAT IS THE MEANING OF THESE MYSTERIOUS MARKINGS?

A NAVAJO NATIVE AMERICAN CARVING FROM NEW MEXICO, U.S.A.

A collection of cup and ring markings are scattered across rugged rocks in Northumberland National Park in Northumberland, England.

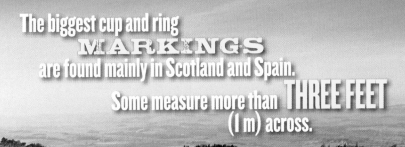

The biggest cup and ring **MARKINGS** are found mainly in Scotland and Spain. Some measure more than **THREE FEET** (1 m) across.

THE BACKGROUND

IMAGINE YOU'RE OUT FOR A WALK and you sit down on a plain old rock to take a rest. Then, as you look more closely, you see it's not plain after all. It's carved with a set of rings, each one inside the next, with a deep hollow carved in the middle. You don't know what it means, but it looks really, really old.

What you've found is a cup and ring mark, and many ordinary people have stumbled upon these incredible finds. There are cup and ring carvings on stones all over Scotland, Ireland, Spain, Scandinavia, and many other parts of Europe. And archaeologists have found similar designs in other places, too: in rock art in Australia, India, Brazil, Mexico, Malawi, Mozambique, and North and South America. A rock called the Reinhardt Boulder, in the state of Georgia, U.S.A., has very old markings that look almost exactly like cup and ring carvings from Dingle, Ireland. Is that a coincidence, or is there a stranger explanation?

Scientists have analyzed cup and ring marks and found that the oldest are 8,000 years old. Some date back to Neolithic times (more than 5,000 years ago), when ancient peoples also built stone circles and burial mounds. So what could the curious design mean?

THE DETAILS

CUP AND RING MARKS are often found high up on a hill, surrounded by long-distance views. There can be just one, or lots of them on one rock. Often, they're on flat or gently sloping stones. And sometimes, old, worn-out patterns have newer ones carved on top—showing that these same spots stayed important for long periods of time.

THE CLUES

There are still a lot of questions to be answered about cup and ring carvings. But there are a few useful clues out there, too.

CUPS OF WATER The marks often overlook lakes, rivers, or other bodies of water. And the "cups" in the middle sometimes fill up with rainwater. When you think about it, the designs look kind of watery, too, like ripples in a pond. Do they have something to do with water rituals or beliefs?

GIANT VERSIONS In the Golan Heights in the Middle East, there's an ancient monument, Rujm el-Hiri. Though much bigger, it's spookily similar to a cup and ring pattern when seen from the air. So are some Stone Age monuments, like Stonehenge, a ring of standing stones.

OFF TO THE NEXT LIFE? Cup and ring patterns also resemble passage tombs, circular Stone Age burial mounds with a tunnel leading into the middle. And what's more, these tombs often have cup and ring marks carved into the stones they're built from.

Rujm-el-Hiri, a 5,000-year-old stone monument in the Middle East with a cup-and-ring-shaped design

A DESIGN RESEMBLING CUP AND RING MARKS NEAR ST. GEORGE, UTAH, U.S.A.

CUP-AND-RING-STYLE CARVINGS AT NEWGRANGE

THE THEORIES

THERE ARE *LOTS* OF THEORIES about cup and ring marks. Dozens of them, in fact! They range from seriously scientific to fantastically freaky.

Were the carvings made by aliens? Are they pictures of flying saucers? Could they be channeling mysterious energy from place to place, or were they hangouts for fairies? Since the same patterns appear in many places around the world, did early people cross the oceans thousands of years earlier than we think they did? Or is it just that a set of circles is a basic pattern that many different cultures thought up independently?

Maybe the carvings marked the territory of a particular group or village. Perhaps they pointed the way to water sources. Or maybe people believed that water that collected in the cups was sacred and they used it for religious ceremonies.

Some experts say the carvings are maps of the planets and sun made by early astronomers. That could be why cup and ring markings are often found on hilltops.

Then there's this theory: Cup and ring stones look similar to ancient stone circles and burial mounds. Some think they must be symbols of these things, which were very important to Stone Age people. According to one theory, the cup in the middle of the design symbolized a sacred "gateway," where people's souls passed through into the afterlife. It doesn't get much more important than that!

With all these ideas to choose from, it's no wonder the puzzle hasn't been solved. So, look out next time you go for a hike—you could be the one to stumble across a new clue!

WHAT COULD THESE CURIOUS CARVINGS MEAN?

Scientists have found that **10 PERCENT** of the Scottish men today are **DESCENDED** from the Picts.

Pictish carvings on a stone at Crichie Henge in Scotland, featuring an example of the "Pictish beast" at the top

THE BACKGROUND

TWO THOUSAND YEARS AGO, the ancient Romans conquered many parts of northern Africa, western Asia, and Europe. But when they tried to take over Scotland, in the north of Britain, they hit a problem: a bunch of scary, super tough warriors who refused to back down. They were so stubborn and fierce that the Romans gave up on most of Scotland and retreated back south.

The Irish called these people the Cruithini, meaning "people of the designs." And Roman writers such as Eumenius called them the Picti or Picts, thought to describe their painted or tattooed skin. It seems the Picts were into body art and may have covered their skin with patterns or pictures to make themselves look terrifying in battle.

But much about these fierce fighters of the north remains a mystery. We don't know what name they called themselves, where they came from, or why, around A.D. 900, they seemed to vanish from history.

All that's left of Pictish culture is a few ruined forts and pieces of jewelry—and, scattered across northern and eastern Scotland, hundreds of stones carved with mysterious animals, humans, and abstract shapes. What were they for, and what did they mean? Could the carvings hold the key to who the Picts really were—if we could understand them?

EUROPE

AFRICA

Where the Picts lived

ATLANTIC OCEAN

SCOTLAND

North Sea

N. IRELAND

UNITED KINGDOM

ENGLAND

IRELAND

75

THE DETAILS

THE PICTISH STONE CARVINGS include some familiar features. The swirling artistic style is similar to Celtic art, also found in Scotland. A few of the stones have short inscriptions in Ogham, an old Irish form of writing. And some include Christian crosses, as Christianity came to Scotland during Pictish times. But most of the images—strange beasts, unidentified people, and a set of over 30 geometric symbols—have not been seen anywhere else on Earth.

THE CLUES
When they took a closer look, experts found that many of the same mysterious markings cropped up again and again. What could this mean?

- **PICTISH PICTURE PATTERNS?** The Pictish carvings are full of pictures but not scenes or landscapes. The same animals, objects, and shapes appear over and over, on different stones, often in pairs or patterns.

- **A BAFFLING BEAST** One peculiar animal, known as the Pictish Beast, appears many times in Pictish carvings—but what is it, and why is it so common? It's been described as a seahorse, a dolphin, a dragon, a swimming elephant, a deer, a whale, or even the Loch Ness Monster.

- **THE PICTISH TONGUE** In the A.D. 700s, the monk and historian Bede wrote that the Picts had their own language. Another writer, Adomnán, described how Irish monk Saint Columba, who spread Christianity to Scotland, couldn't understand the Pictish people, as their language was so different from others in Scotland.

THE THEORIES

STONES LAST FOR CENTURIES, whereas paper, fabrics, and wooden objects are more likely to be destroyed or rot away over time. The Pictish

One of the best-preserved carved stones, known as Aberlemno 1, whose carvings including a serpent, a mirror, and a comb

designs that survive are now mostly on stone, but experts think the Picts probably used them on other surfaces too.

For example, maybe they painted their bodies with the same images. One theory is that an animal or symbol could have stood for a particular tribe or leader. Or the images could have represented useful qualities, such as a serpent for stealth, or a wolf for fierceness.

We may never know what animal the Pictish Beast is, but we might be able to figure out

its meaning. Some experts think it could have stood for a rank in society, such as a tribal leader. This would explain why it is found on stones from many different areas.

On the other hand, the animal carving known as the Burghead Bull is found only on stones dug up at a Pictish fort at Burghead in northern Scotland. The bull could have been the symbol of that fort or of a Pictish clan or tribe from that area.

In 2010, a new theory made a big splash. A team of scientists studied the symbols and found that the images often appeared together in the same sequences, just as letters do in words. So, they claimed, the carved symbols were actually the letters of an alphabet spelling out words in an unknown language—the long-lost language of the Picts!

Others disagreed, and experts are still debating whether this could be true. To prove it, the language would have to be decoded, and for that, we'd need a longer piece of writing, like a Pictish book or letter. Until someone finds one, the symbols will stay shrouded in secrecy ... so we'd better keep looking!

• THE CASE •
ANCIENT ALIENS

DOES ANCIENT ART SHOW VISITORS FROM OUTER SPACE?

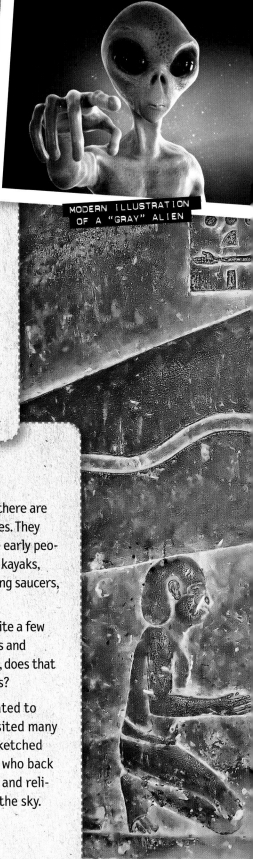

MODERN ILLUSTRATION OF A "GRAY" ALIEN

THE BACKGROUND

ALL OVER THE WORLD, in almost every country and continent, there are cave paintings and rock carvings that survive from ancient times. They reveal all kinds of interesting information about the lives of the early people who made them. They show things like animal hunts, dances, kayaks, people collecting honey—and aliens landing from the sky in flying saucers, rounding up a few humans, and carting them off into space.

Hang on ... What? Well, as you'll see on these pages, there are quite a few examples of ancient rock art that really do resemble astronauts and spaceships. Since most of this type of art shows real-life scenes, does that mean visits from aliens actually happened back in ancient times?

Some writers and ufologists, or people who study things related to UFOs, claim that in the distant past, "ancient astronauts" visited many parts of the world. They say people at the time would have sketched these events on their cave walls. Besides the pictures, those who back the alien theory point to the fact that many myths, legends, and religions around the world involve magical beings visiting from the sky. Could those beliefs actually be based on alien encounters?

78

Why do some ancient carvings depict things that resemble modern-day objects—things like lightbulbs and helicopters—that were invented long after these civilizations came and went?

In Hindu mythology, **THE GODS** travel around the sky in flying vehicles called **Vimanas**. Some people think these must have been alien **FLYING SAUCERS!**

THE DETAILS

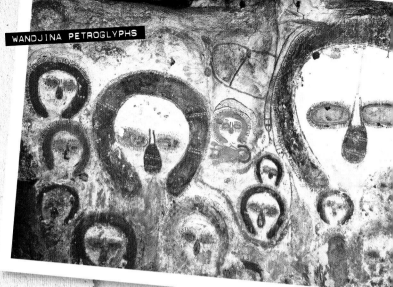

WANDJINA PETROGLYPHS

ANCIENT "ALIEN" ROCK ART is scattered across a wide variety of locations: Australia, northern Africa, Italy, North and South America, India, and China, to name a few. All of it dates back several thousand years, and some of the artworks were created as early as 10,000 years ago. That's even earlier than most ancient civilizations, such as those from ancient Egypt. These people would have used hard stones to engrave their pictures into softer rock, or painted artworks using pigments made from colored clay called ochre.

THE CLUES

Flying saucers and rockets, astronauts in protective suits, sci-fi ray guns, and even almond-eyed aliens: They can all be found on old rocks if you know where to look ...

- **SPOOKY SPACE SUITS** The "ancient astronaut" theory gets its name from figures that look as if they're wearing space suits. One carving in Val Camonica, Italy, shows two people who appear to be in white suits with spike-covered helmets, carrying weird gadgets. Meanwhile, cave paintings from Tassili-n-Ajjer, Algeria, depict humanoid figures with their faces covered with ball-like helmets.

- **UFOs FROM LONG AGO** Rock paintings discovered in Charama, India, and Xinjiang, China, include things that look just like flying saucers and spaceships from a sci-fi movie. One of the "astronauts" at Tassili-n-Ajjer has what appears to be a flying saucer in the sky behind him or her, while another Tassili picture shows a row of people being led into a strange round object.

- **BIG-EYED ALIENS** In Kimberley, Australia, Aboriginal rock art shows the Wandjina, sky spirits with pointed faces and huge oval eyes. Legends say the Wandjina came from space and created humans long ago. Far away in Utah, U.S.A., spookily similar beings appear in the cave paintings of the Anasazi people, showing the "star people," who they believed brought life to Earth.

THE THEORIES

WHEN YOU SEE an old cave painting that looks like a flying saucer, it's pretty exciting! It's easy to be drawn in by the idea that art like this is a record of ancient alien landings. But if it's true, why did aliens come here so often in the ancient past?

Supporters of the ancient astronaut theory say aliens came to help humans. They may have shown them useful technology or helped them build monuments. In fact, some argue that early humans couldn't have built structures like Stonehenge or the Pyramids at Giza on their own, so aliens must have helped them! This would also explain why wondrous beings from the sky appear in so many creation myths and religious texts.

Rock art in Sego Canyon, Utah, shows these alien-like creatures with enormous eyes.

What's more, people who claim to have seen aliens often say they have pointed faces and huge slanted eyes—a type of extraterrestrial known as a "grey." The rock art "aliens" often look strangely similar.

But let's not get carried away! Most scientists and rock art experts don't agree with the theory. They point out that ancient people weren't any less intelligent than modern ones and they had a lot of clever technology and building methods. Even if we haven't yet discovered how they did something, that doesn't mean they didn't do it.

It's also well known that when we see an image, we match it to our own experience. To us, a cave painting might look like a UFO, or an alien from TV or a cartoon. But that doesn't mean it would have meant the same thing to the artist who made it. It could actually be a crazy head-dress, a monster from a story, a house, a star, or just a cool pattern. Or maybe those ancient people were simply making up their own sci-fi stories, just as we do today!

IS THERE LIFE ON NEIGHBORING PLANETS?

It would be hard to survive on the surface of **MARS,** as the temperature swings from warm during the day (up to 70°F, or 20°C) to way below **FREEZING** at night (as cold as -200°F, or -130°C).

Perspective view of Melas Chasma, a large canyon on Mars, based on satellite data.

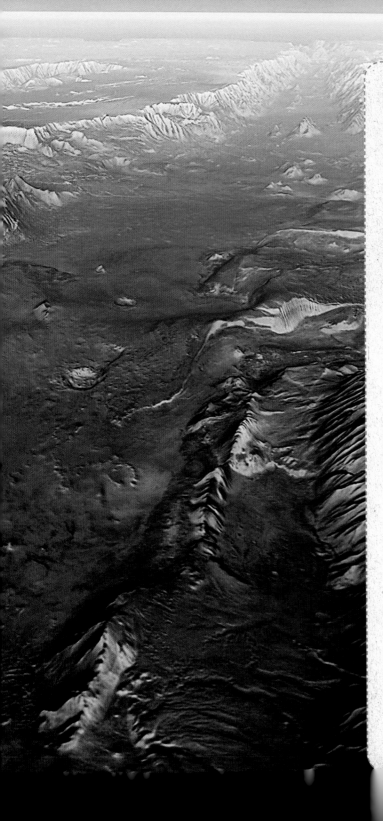

THE BACKGROUND

MARS, a planet that's one of Earth's closest neighbors, is often easy to spot in the night sky, and it has fascinated humans since ancient times. It's nicknamed the "red planet" because its surface dust contains a lot of reddish, rusty iron, giving it a red glow. In the 1600s, early astronomers found that Mars has icy poles like the Earth and that it spins and rotates around the sun, giving it days and seasons. Since Mars seemed so similar to Earth, they reasoned it might also be home to living things. The search for Martians has been on ever since!

In the 1800s, one astronomer named Percival Lowell thought that patterns of straight lines spotted on Mars could be canals built by intelligent beings. In 1976, a photo taken by the Viking 1 space probe showed a rock that looked amazingly like a face—maybe some kind of Martian monument? Sadly for UFO fans, further investigations showed both of these were just random patterns and shadows. But we're still looking! Since the 1970s, scientists have sent more than a dozen orbiters, landers, and rovers to the red planet to explore the surface. They continue to turn up exciting evidence that sends alien hunters into a frenzy.

THE DETAILS

AS FAR AS WE KNOW, in order for life to exist, there must be liquid water in the environment. That's how you and the rest of life on Earth can survive—because we have plenty of H_2O. On Mars, the low-pressure atmosphere and extreme temperatures mean that water is mainly either frozen or vaporized into gas. But signs of liquid water could mean that life is possible there—or perhaps existed in the past.

THE "FACE ON MARS" WAS SPOTTED BY THE VIKING 1 PROBE IN 1976.

THE CLUES
The more closely space probes investigate the red planet, the more exciting evidence they uncover. Each time a new clue appears, the world wonders what it could mean ...

CURIOUS CHANNELS In 1971, Mariner 9 became the first spacecraft from Earth to orbit Mars, taking pictures and making maps and measurements. The pioneering probe blew scientists away when it revealed that the planet's surface was carved with deep channels and hollows.

STRANGE STREAKS Since the 1990s, close-up photos of the Martian surface have revealed strange dark streaks. They lead away from ridges and crater rims, suggesting something is running or flowing downhill.

THE CHEMICALS OF LIFE? In 2014, NASA announced that its Curiosity rover, which landed on Mars in 2012, had discovered organic chemicals such as methane and chlorobenzene. Organic chemicals contain the element carbon and are often found in and made by living things.

MARS CURIOSITY ROVER

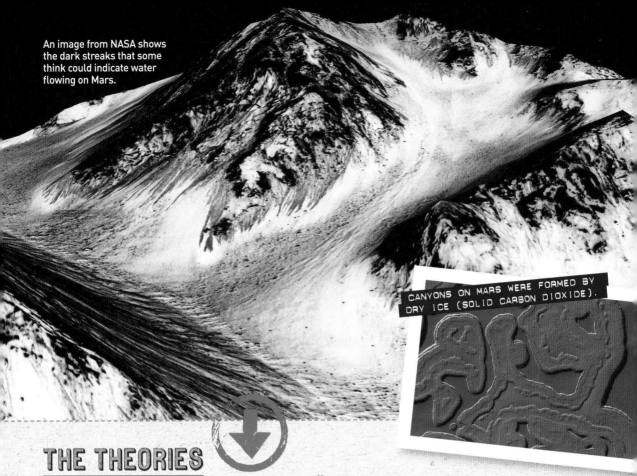

An image from NASA shows the dark streaks that some think could indicate water flowing on Mars.

CANYONS ON MARS WERE FORMED BY DRY ICE (SOLID CARBON DIOXIDE).

THE THEORIES

ASTRONOMERS SOON REALIZED that the channels and hollows on Mars looked freakily familiar. They were just like the river and lake beds on our own planet—except with no water in them. And that's exactly what they were! Scientists determined that water once flowed on the surface of Mars, carving channels into the rocks as it does on Earth. But what about now—is Mars still soggy enough to support life, or is it as dry as a bone? Some of the scientists who studied the dark streaks claimed they could be caused by ice melting, creating downhill water flows. But others disagreed, saying they were just flows of loose dust.

As for the organic chemicals, they don't mean there's definitely life on Mars, as there are other ways they could have formed—for example, they could have been the result of different minerals mixing together. But it's another tantalizing piece of the puzzle.

The more evidence we find for water on Mars, the greater the chance that some kind of Martian does, or did, exist. But there's no sign so far of intelligent civilizations—no buildings or technology, and definitely no canals! So if we do discover life, it will almost certainly be something small and simple, similar to our Earth bacteria.

Whatever it may be, space scientists aren't giving up the search. They're planning more missions to Mars in the future, including the first with humans on board. The universe is so huge, it's overwhelmingly likely that alien life does exist somewhere—so we might as well look close to home!

HELICOPTER HIEROGLYPHICS

CURIOUS **CARVINGS** OF FLYING **MACHINES** IN AN **ANCIENT EGYPTIAN** TEMPLE

The temple of the pharaoh
Seti I in Abydos, Egypt

THE BACKGROUND

IMAGINE YOU'RE an adventurous archaeological explorer investigating the inside of an ancient Egyptian temple. As you shine your flashlight around the walls and ceilings, you marvel at carvings of birds and snakes, hieroglyphics—ancient Egyptian symbols—recording the reigns of great kings and queens, and ... a helicopter, a glider, a rocket ship, and a submarine!?

Did the ancient Egyptians have these things? Not as far as we know! So it's more than a little strange that these modern modes of transportation were seemingly used to decorate the temple of Pharaoh Seti I. Seti built his fabulous temple in the ancient city of Abydos—around 3,300 years ago—to show off his importance as Egypt's ruler. The peculiar pictures, known as the "helicopter hieroglyphics," make up just a small section of the temple's many reliefs, or carved pictures, but as you can imagine, they have caused a huge stir.

When a photo of the helicopter hieroglyphics was circulated on the internet, some people claimed it proved the ancient Egyptians were a lot more advanced than we thought and actually had their own aircraft. Others said the ancient art must mean that aliens visited the Egyptians in spaceships. It's even been claimed the pictures could show modern aircraft that somehow time-traveled to the past.

It might sound crazy—but when you see the pictures, they really do look weirdly like modern technology. How could that happen?

87

THE DETAILS

PHARAOH SETI I started work on the temple during his reign in the 1200s B.C. It was completed by his son, Ramses II, when he came to power. The curious carvings aren't very easy to spot at first: They're small in size and positioned high up on a roof support in the temple. The reliefs on the support include pictures, hieroglyphics, and cartouches, which are oval panels containing royal names.

THE CLUES

The ancient Egyptians were certainly smart, and they achieved a lot of amazing things ... but flying machines? Really? We need to take a closer look ...

MODERN MACHINES One of the strangest things about the aircraft pictures is how modern they look. The style doesn't seem very ancient Egyptian: It's more like a set of 21st-century logos or cartoons. The helicopter has a pointed nose, making it resemble a well-known modern helicopter, the Westland Lynx.

EVIDENCE IS EVERYWHERE Those who think the carvings really do show aircraft say that this isn't the only example of modern technology cropping up in ancient Egypt. They point to the Dendera light, a relief showing a strange object that some see as a lightbulb. Meanwhile, the Saqqara bird, a model bird found in an Egyptian tomb, has wings and a tail similar to those on today's airplanes.

THE CLUE'S IN THE NAME! Let's not forget the name of the king who founded the temple—none other than Seti I. Today, SETI is short for the "search for extraterrestrial intelligence," and it's the name of a modern scientific organization devoted to—you guessed it—tracking down aliens. UFO believers claim that can't be a coincidence!

SETI I

THE THEORIES

THE HELICOPTER HIEROGLYPHS may look convincing ... but as you've learned by now, even the oddest occurrences can have rational explanations. And if you ask Egyptologists (experts on ancient Egypt), they'll tell you exactly that.

Pharaoh Ramses II, son of Seti, was a very powerful ruler, and he liked people to know it. So he often covered the names of previous kings on carvings and temples with his own. According to the experts, that's what happened when Ramses completed Seti's temple. The panel in question had been carved with hieroglyphs spelling out a flattering description of the great Seti I. Not to be outdone by his dad, Ramses had this carving filled in with plaster and replaced with a description of himself, using different hieroglyphs. Over time, some of the plaster fell out, leaving a mash-up of both carvings. This, the experts explain, created the odd shapes which, to us, look like flying machines.

What's more, the photo that went viral on the web had been digitally altered. In real life, the panel looks messier, and you can see how some hieroglyphs have been carved on top of others.

But those who want to believe in ancient aliens aren't convinced, and they claim it's all a cover-up. They say it's pretty weird that some messy, mixed-up writing would create not just one but four modern-day vehicles, all in one tiny area. What are the chances? They believe the only explanation must be that the Egyptians, in some unexplained way or another, had access to the best high-tech future transportation technology. Well, when they find a carving of a jet pack, maybe we'll be convinced!

An unfiltered close-up look at the strangely modern-looking carvings. Can you spot the helicopter, submarine (or tank), spaceship, and glider?

THE BAFFLING DESERT BOULDERS THAT MOVE THEMSELVES

ONE OF THE SAILING STONES

THE BACKGROUND

1 **THE ROCK IN THIS PICTURE** is sitting on Racetrack Playa, a dry lake bed in Death Valley National Park in California, U.S.A. It has a strange trail behind it in the mud, making it look as if the rock has been wandering around on its own. The weird thing is, it has!

Yep—these boulders, known as the "sailing stones," really do move across the lake bed, baffling scientists and sightseers alike. What could be going on? The tracks lead in a range of random directions and sometimes turn corners, so they weren't caused by the stones rolling downhill. Do people sneak out at night and shift them around? If so, they don't leave footprints. And the stones—more than 60 of them—have been moving for at least a hundred years, since they were first reported in the early 1900s. No one would carry on a hoax for that long!

THE DETAILS

[2] RACETRACK PLAYA is a large, dried-up lake bed that's almost completely flat. The sailing stones got there when wind and weather wore away at the surrounding mountains until the stones broke off and fell onto the playa. They range from small rocks the size of your fist to much bigger boulders weighing up to 700 pounds (320 kg). Some move more than others, with the longest tracks measuring more than 1,500 feet (450 m). And although it's very hard to catch the rocks in action, it's clear that most of the movements happen in winter.

THE THEORIES

[3] WHAT COULD BE moving the stones? Of course, it wasn't long before ufologists suggested it could be aliens, perhaps trying to leave us some kind of spooky message from space. But scientists also came up with lots of other ideas. Some thought perhaps magnetic forces were moving the stones, but tests for magnetism in the area turned up nothing. Others thought the culprit could be desert whirlwinds called dust devils, or high-speed storm winds. But calculations showed that even a hurricane-force wind couldn't blow a huge, heavy rock out of place.

TRACKS OF THE SAILING STONES

North

NEW EVIDENCE REVEALED!

IN 2006, a scientist named Ralph Lorenz started studying the mystery of the sailing stones. He knew that ice has sometimes been known to move rocks from the sea onto the shore—but only when the ice floats on top of water. He made a model by trapping a pebble in a piece of ice, then floating the ice in a tray of shallow water. Just a small breeze was enough to move it along. Lorenz had discovered how the rocks

rainfall, when the playa is covered in a thin layer of water, ice freezes around the stones. The rock-toting ice sheets float on a layer of water underneath. That lifts the stones enough for them to drift along in the wind, scraping a trail into the mud as they go. Over the next few years, time-lapse cameras and satellite tracking finally recorded it happening. No aliens needed!

5

MYSTERIOUS RUINS

Inside the Temple of Bacchus
at the mysterious ancient site
of Baalbek in Lebanon

WE'VE BEEN EXPLORING our world for a long time. So you might think we know all there is to know about the ruins that remain from the ancient past. In fact, though, all kinds of wrecks and relics still baffle archaeologists. And what's more, we keep finding new ones that are even harder to understand! Some date from so long ago, it seems impossible that anyone in those days could have built them—and ancient legends claim their creators were supernatural! Some contain mysterious carvings and writings that no one has managed to decipher. And some are said to be the places where legendary events actually happened. Follow the clues to see which monumental mysteries we can solve, and which strange secrets are still lost to time.

WHO *MOVED* THE WORLD'S BIGGEST BUILDING BLOCKS AND HOW?

ANCIENT ROMAN RUINS AT BAALBEK

Baalbek's **TEMPLE OF JUPITER** looks amazing today, with its six supersize **COLUMNS**– but when it was first built, it had 54 of them!

96

The six remaining mighty columns
of Baalbek's Temple of Jupiter

THE BACKGROUND

IN THE BEKAA VALLEY in Lebanon stands one of the most mysterious and mind-boggling ancient ruins in the world: the Roman temple complex of Baalbek.

When the Romans decided to build here, they really went to town. They spent almost 300 years constructing walls, courtyards, grand staircases, and incredible temples. The largest, the Temple of Jupiter, was the biggest temple in the whole Roman empire, with columns a staggering 70 feet (21 m) tall—the height of a seven-story building!

But the towering temple isn't the most amazing thing about Baalbek. What's really weird is what the temple stands on: a huge platform the size of a soccer field and 23 feet (7 m) high. It's built from stones so impossibly large, no one can figure out how they got there. Yet they are perfectly rectangular, neatly arranged blocks, which someone must have cut into shape and moved into place.

A curator of the ruins once wrote, "No description will give an idea of the bewildering and stupefying effect of these tremendous blocks on the spectator." In other words, when you see them, they blow your mind!

How could the Romans have moved these mega–building blocks, many times the size of those used in Stonehenge, so neatly into place? Or was the platform already there when they arrived—and if so, who built it?

EUROPE
ASIA
LEBANON—
AFRICA

Mediterranean Sea
LEBANON
Bekaa Valley
Baalbek
SYRIA
ISRAEL

THE DETAILS

THE THREE BIGGEST STONES making up the platform at Baalbek are known as the "trilithon" (meaning "three stones"). These stones are around 65 feet (20 m) long, 15 feet (4.5 m) tall, and 10 feet (3 m) thick, and they weigh an estimated 880 tons (800 t) each. Even today, engineers have a hard time shifting something this heavy.

We do know that the stones didn't have to travel far. They came from a quarry less than a mile (1.6 km) away, where archaeologists have found other, similar stones still half-stuck in the ground, in the process of being quarried. Maybe whoever built the platform was planning to make it even bigger but didn't finish the job.

THE CLUES
There are plenty of myths and legends about Baalbek, and archaeologists have spent many years studying the stones. Are they any closer to the truth?

THESE STONES DON'T MATCH! Many observers have pointed out that the giant stones in the platform don't look much like the smaller stones used to build the Temple of Jupiter above them. They also seem more weathered and worn, as if they've been there for longer.

WHAT'S THIS DRUM DOING HERE? According to a 1975 book about Baalbek, archaeologists discovered a cylindrical piece of stone, called a "drum" in the ground under the platform. It seemed to be a section of stone like the ones used to build the temple's columns.

GIANT OF A TALE According to a local legend about the site, Nimrod, the great-grandson of Noah, biblical builder of the Ark, constructed the massive monument after the biblical flood. He had a handy team of giants to move the huge stones.

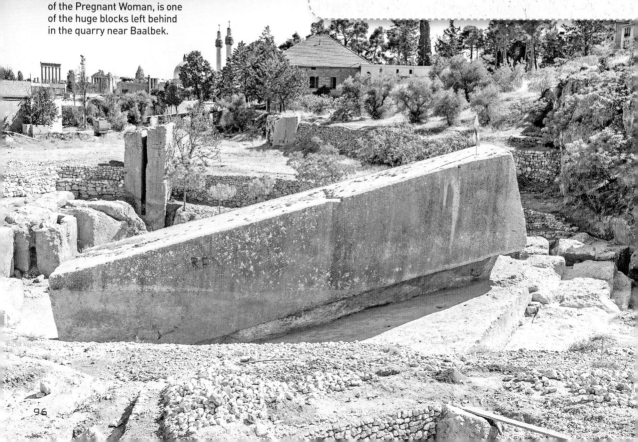

This stone, named the Stone of the Pregnant Woman, is one of the huge blocks left behind in the quarry near Baalbek.

THE THEORIES

BAALBEK HAS BEEN INHABITED for thousands of years, and it was a holy place for other cultures before the Romans arrived. It's named after Baal, the sky god of the ancient Phoenicians. According to legend, Baal came down to Earth from the sky—prompting believers of the alien theory to claim that the story must have originated when an ancient alien visited Earth. The platform at Baalbek was actually a humongous helipad, they say, which these aliens built as a landing spot for their spacecraft.

But what about the giants in local stories? It's quite common for people to think that giants or magical beings must have built ancient monuments. While there's no evidence for this, these local legends are very old and might indicate that the ruins do date back to before the Romans. Perhaps the Phoenicians themselves had a way of moving the stones. Or maybe it was the ancient Egyptians, since they had experience with moving big stones (though not this big!) when they built the pyramids.

Despite all these ideas, most archaeologists think the Romans probably built Baalbek. Famous for their architectural skills, they were the most likely people to have mastered a method for moving massive stones. The weird thing is, although the Romans kept detailed written histories, their books contain no mention of the building of Baalbek. And no one knows why they used such big stones when smaller ones would have been easier. One theory is that they simply wanted to show off their genius and strength to the people in their empire.

But how did they move them? Did they float them on a canal, roll them on giant wheels, or use an army of thousands to drag them? All of these options would all have been nightmarishly difficult. It's still a baffling brain-bender ... and it makes Baalbek a magnet for mystery-loving tourists.

SEARCHING
MAZE
FOR THE   OF THE
MONSTROUS
MINOTAUR

A MAZE-LIKE PATTERN FROM KNOSSOS, GREECE

THE BACKGROUND

MANY MYSTERIES surround the ancient people known as the Minoans, a seagoing, super-advanced culture that dominated the Mediterranean area around 2000 B.C. They had a written language, but we can't figure it out. By 1450 B.C., their society had collapsed, but we're not sure why. Even though we call them the Minoans, we don't even know what they called themselves! The name Minoans came from archaeologist Arthur Evans. He named them after Minos, an early king of the island of Crete in Greek legends.

King Minos was one of the most bloodthirsty mythical Greeks. After a falling-out with the city of Athens, Minos forced the Athenians to send him seven boys and seven girls every nine years as food for the flesh-hungry Minotaur. The Minotaur was Minos's son, a half-man, half-bull monster. He was so dangerous that he was kept in a labyrinth, or maze, that was impossible to escape.

Arthur Evans unearthed the palace of Knossos on Crete in 1900 and discovered a multilevel building with endless rooms and corridors, especially on the basement level. Newspapers reported that the real labyrinth of the Minotaur had been found. But had it?

In Greek mythology, the hero **THESEUS** used a ball of yarn—given to him by Minos's daughter Ariadne—to keep **TRACK OF HIS PATH** through the maze and find his way out again.

An artist's depiction of Greek hero Theseus facing off against the mighty Minotaur

THE DETAILS

KNOSSOS DEFINITELY DOES have one heck of a big basement, but archaeologists have pointed out that it doesn't seem deliberately designed as a maze. It's more like a warren of food storage cupboards, craft workshops, and servants' quarters. There's also evidence that the palace was built in several stages. The Minoans may have filled in and built on top of older, lower rooms when they added new parts.

Was King Minos a real person? It's possible, as Greek legends were often based on people and events from hundreds of years earlier.

However, it seems less likely that he really kept a monster in a maze. How could this story have come about?

THE CLUES
Evidence from Minoan ruins such as the palace of Knossos reveals tantalizing details about how these ancient people really lived.

BONKERS FOR BULLS! Whether or not they had a bull-headed beast in the basement, the Minoans were obsessed with bulls. They had frescoes (wall paintings), pottery, and sculptures. These often show bull-leaping, a scary sport involving grabbing a bull's horns and flipping yourself right over its back!

THE TWO-HEADED AXE A type of two-headed ceremonial axe was also important to the Minoans. They're often seen in Minoan ruins and wall art. The ancient Greeks called this type of axe a *labrys*.

MINOAN MAZE ART Even if the basement of Knossos was not an actual labyrinth, the Minoans were interested in mazes. A faint pattern that looks like a map of a maze appears on the walls at Knossos.

THE RUINS OF THE PALACE OF KNOSSOS

A LATER ROMAN MOSAIC SHOWING THE LABYRINTH WITH THE GREEK HERO THESEUS AND THE MINOTAUR

MINOAN AXE

FRESCO DEPICTING BULL-LEAPING

THE THEORIES

THE LEGENDS ABOUT King Minos developed long after the Minoan civilization ended. Like many myths, the story probably changed as it was told and retold, becoming more exciting and supernatural. The man-eating Minotaur could be a Greek invention, as it's similar to other mixed-up creatures in Greek legends, like Pegasus the winged horse, or Medusa, who had snakes for hair. The myth could also have been influenced by the ancient Egyptians, who had a whole host of animal-headed gods.

The Minoans may also have made sacrifices to a bull god—possibly even human sacrifices. Maybe they did have a war with Athens and took young Athenians to sacrifice to the bull god. In Athens, this could have ended up as a story about their children being eaten by a bull-like monster.

But what about the labyrinth? The Minoans' double-headed axe, or *labrys*, could hold the key. In Greek myths, an inventor named Daedalus built the labyrinth for Minos. But when the Greeks used the word "labyrinth," they may have just meant "house of the labrys," in honor of the Minoans' favorite weapon. In other words, all Daedalus was building was a regular palace at Knossos. Later, the word "labyrinth" came to mean a maze.

However, maybe Minos did have his own maze after all. Ask locals where the labyrinth is, and they'll point you to Gortyn, 20 miles (32 km) to the south. This is the site of a series of winding underground tunnels and rooms called the Labyrinthos Caves. Since Knossos became famous, they've been mostly ignored. But recently, some archaeologists have explored them, and they say they could be the actual "labyrinth" in the story.

Maybe Minos used it as a dungeon. Or, if he really did have a Minotaur, this would have been a better place for the terrible monster than in his own basement!

WHAT **ARE** THE STRANGE STONE STRUCTURES OF "BELLY HILL"?

THE BACKGROUND

IN 1963, an archaeologist stumbled across a few stone tools and rocky slabs on a hill in Turkey. It was no surprise, as there were Stone Age ruins nearby. But he thought the slabs were more recent gravestones, so he left the hill alone. Little did he know it contained a mind-blowing secret.

About 30 years later, German archaeologist Klaus Schmidt explored the site. He thought the smooth, rounded hill, named Göbekli Tepe (or "Belly Hill") looked human-made. And when he and his team began to excavate, they discovered something astonishing.

The flat slabs in the ground weren't gravestones, but the tops of tall carved stone shapes. Inside the hill stood an ancient structure with circular walls and rings of T-shaped pillars. They were covered with mysterious symbols and pictures of animals such as snakes, foxes, scorpions, spiders, and vultures. In fact, the whole area turned out to be dotted with other, similar buildings—at least 20 of them.

EUROPE
ASIA
TURKEY
AFRICA

BULGARIA   Black Sea

GREECE

TURKEY
Göbekli Tepe

SYRIA

Mediterranean Sea

It was an amazing discovery, revealing a type of building never seen before. The pillars and carvings baffled experts. But the most incredible thing about Göbekli Tepe is its age: Carbon dating shows it was built 11,000 years ago. That's old—really old. It's 6,000 years older than Egypt's Great Pyramid, and the earliest writing on Sumerian tablets. It dates from a prehistoric time when all humans were thought to be hunter-gatherers, incapable of big building projects. How did they do it ... and why?

The ruins of Göbekli Tepe by night, after being excavated

Before **GÖBEKLI TEPE** was evacuated, the hill was used for **FARMING.** Some of the T-shaped pillars have been damaged by farmers' plows and shovels.

THE DETAILS

GÖBEKLI TEPE is on a high plateau in southern Turkey, near a mountain range, and surrounded by plains and valleys. Today it's a desertlike area, but 11,000 years ago, it was green and fertile, with more wildlife. From Göbekli Tepe, people would have been able to look out over the lands where they went hunting and foraging for food.

The circular structures range from 33 to 100 feet (10–30 m) across. The pillars stand up to 16 feet (5 m) tall and weigh up to 20,000 pounds (9,000 kg). More of these pillars have been found in the ground nearby, half cut out of the rock. This shows that people carved them out of the stone then dragged them into place.

THE CLUES

Göbekli Tepe is so unlike anything else that archaeologists have had to start from scratch trying to figure out what it was for. Could these clues help them crack it?

CURIOUS CARVINGS Prehistoric art usually shows animals that ancient humans hunted for food. But the Göbekli Tepe carvings depict predators and dangerous animals such as snakes and scorpions. Some of the pillars also have arms carved onto the sides, suggesting they are human figures.

COVERED UP Like many ruins, Göbekli Tepe was buried underground—but not accidentally. It seemed to have been deliberately filled and covered over with rubble in ancient times.

BAFFLING BONES Archaeologists have found lots of bone fragments at the site. Many are animal bones, but some are human, including fragments of skulls with mysterious lines carved into them.

The quarry the stones came from, with another humongous stone halfway out of the ground

THE THEORIES

BECAUSE THE STONES are so large and heavy, some people are convinced the only way ancient people could have built Göbekli Tepe was with the help of aliens! To support this theory, they say the buildings in the area are arranged to represent constellations. There's also a theory that one of the carved pillars, known as the "vulture stone," shows a comet that passed by the Earth around the time Göbekli Tepe was built.

However, we know from modern re-creations that it is possible to cut and move large stones using basic technology like flint tools, ramps, and ropes. What's really puzzling is that it would have taken hundreds of workers, with well-organized planning and leadership, to make it happen. Previously, experts thought that people at this point in history only lived in small groups and didn't carry out big building projects.

According to one theory, the buildings were houses, with the pillars holding up wooden roof beams covered with layers of rubble and soil for warmth. The buildings could have been buried when these roofs eventually collapsed. But it would have been a huge effort to cut, move, and carve stone pillars just to make a house. Perhaps this was the palace of someone important, like an ancient king or queen? That seems unlikely because the site is high up and there's no nearby water source. Living here wouldn't have made much sense. Instead, the site might have been a temple or holy gathering place.

The human bones at the site lead to another possible answer: Perhaps this was a burial place. Many ancient peoples worshipped their ancestors. They could have buried people here or perhaps left their bodies to be picked clean by vultures, a tradition known as a "sky burial." People could then have come here on special occasions to worship their dead. The fierce animals on the pillars may have been put there to ward off danger or evil.

We don't know for sure. What we do know is, these people from long ago were much better builders than we thought. What else could be lying under the soil, waiting to surprise us?

ARCHAEOLOGISTS EXCAVATE AT GÖBEKLI TEPE.

TEMPLE, GRAVEYARD, OR THE WORLD'S OLDEST OBSERVATORY?

The **GOSECK CIRCLE** is at the exact same latitude (distance from the Equator) as the British **STONEHENGE.**

This picture shows how the sun shines through the gateways to the middle of the circle, at sunrise and sunset on the shortest day of winter.

THE BACKGROUND

WHEN THIS SITE was first discovered, people thought it was a crop circle, but not the normal (or paranormal) kind! Instead of crops flattened down to create a pattern, this was a big ring of patchy vegetation on the ground. Archaeologists spotted it in 1991 in an aerial photo of fields near Goseck, Germany. This phenomenon is known as a "crop mark". Crop marks are hard to see from the ground nearby, but can be detected from the air. They are created when something buried underground makes the plants above it grow differently from those around them. The Goseck Circle marked the spot where something big, round, and very old had once been. What could it be?

In 2002, excavation began. As archaeologists dug up the site, they gradually uncovered a huge, round rampart, or earth wall, with a diameter of 246 feet (75 m). Inside that was a ditch, then two rings of postholes, where wooden posts had once stood. In some places, there were gaps in the rings forming gateways.

The archaeologists restored the site and fitted hundreds of new, hand-carved oak poles into the holes to show how it had once looked. The Goseck Circle is now open to the public, and anyone can go and explore it. But what was it? There's evidence of bonfires but no sign of houses in the circle, so it doesn't seem to be a village or a fort. Was it an enclosure for animals? A place of worship? A burial site? Or something even more intriguing?

North Sea
NETH.
BELG.
FRANCE
SWITZ.
GERMANY
Goseck
POLAND
CZECH REP.

GERMANY
EUROPE
AFRICA
ASIA

THE DETAILS

THE CIRCLE DATES to around 4900 B.C.—making it an incredible 7,000 years old. That's older than the stone circles at Stonehenge in England, and so old that we know hardly anything about the people who built it. All we really know about them is that they made zigzag-patterned pottery, which gave them the name "stroke-ornamented ware people" ("ware" meaning "pottery"). Fragments of their pottery have been found across a wide area of central Europe, including at the Goseck Circle. There are many other, similar circles across Europe, but this is one of the biggest and oldest.

THE CLUES

This isn't just a plain old circle of sticks. Archaeologists have found a bunch of clues that suggest it was used for something pretty important ...

SUNUP, SUNDOWN When they're viewed from the middle of the circle, the two gateways line up with the sun as it rises and sets on the winter solstice, the shortest day of the year.

SPOOKY SKELETONS Some pretty spooky ancient bones, both animal and human, have been found around the site. They included a headless human skeleton and human bones with knife marks on them.

SPACE DISK In 1999, there was a discovery just 16 miles (25 km) from Goseck: a beautiful ancient bronze disk decorated with a golden sun, moon, and stars, now known as the "Nebra sky disk." Experts think a band on the side may indicate the summer and winter solstices (the longest and shortest days of the year).

THE SUN AS SEEN THROUGH THE GATEWAY

Tourists visit the newly restored Goseck Circle.

NEBRA SKY DISK

THE THEORIES

MANY ANCIENT CIRCLES around Europe seem to have been designed to align with the solstices. In the case of the Goseck Circle, its design would have helped the people who built it identify the shortest day of the year: December 21 in the Northern Hemisphere. So it works as a handy calendar: When the sun rises and sets through the gateways, you know the shortest day of the year has arrived.

But why was it important to identify the shortest day? The builders of Goseck were probably crop farmers. When the winter solstice arrived, it meant spring and summer were on their way back. A sun observatory like this one would help them plan when to prepare the ground and plant seeds.

The Nebra sky disk is another example of how interested the area's ancient people were in the sun and the solstices. Scientific dating shows that someone buried the disk about 3,600 years ago, but it could have been made much earlier. People may have used the Goseck Circle as a model to make such portable disks marked with the solstices, maybe as ceremonial objects or decorations.

Many ancient people celebrated the solstice with rituals or parties. The circle could have been a temple or gathering place, used for a ceremony or festival in the middle of winter. Sound familiar? The winter solstice is actually the origin of many winter celebrations, including the Roman Saturnalia and the Viking Jól or Yule, which was eventually replaced by the Christian Christmas.

And as for the bones? According to archaeologists, bones with cut marks on them are usually a sign of ritual sacrifice. Maybe these people sacrificed animals—or even humans—to the sun as part of the festivities to try to ensure a good harvest in the year ahead.

So perhaps the Goseck Circle was once no mere structure, but the site of ancient astronomical observations and possibly even human sacrifices. The more evidence turns up, the more it becomes clear that what happened here long ago was at least as spooky as crop circles!

THIS COULD BE THE BIGGEST EGYPTIAN FIND – *EVER!*

AN OLD ILLUSTRATION SHOWING THE PART OF THE LABYRINTH DESCRIBED BY HERODOTUS

THE BACKGROUND

1 **AROUND 2,400 YEARS AGO,** ancient Greek writer Herodotus described visiting an amazing building in Egypt, which he called the "labyrinth." He said it was a temple honoring twelve ancient kings, who had built it as a memorial to themselves and the sacred crocodiles they worshipped.

To say Herodotus was blown away by the labyrinth would be an understatement. "The labyrinth surpasses even the pyramids," he wrote. He described a complex of 1,500 rooms filled with carvings, inscriptions, and paintings. Below them were another 1,500 basement rooms, but visitors were not allowed to see these, as they included the kings' sacred tombs.

Other ancient historians also wrote about the labyrinth, and many of them mentioned its maze-like tunnels. In 1679, German scholar Athanasius Kircher used their descriptions to draw a map of what the temple could have looked like.

But no one knew if it was still standing, or if it was ever real at all.

THE DETAILS

2 **IN 1888,** an archaeologist named William Matthew Flinders Petrie figured out where the labyrinth should be: next to a worn-down pyramid at Hawara, near the town of Shedyet or Crocodopolis, where the Egyptians had worshipped the crocodile god Sobek.

Petrie did some excavating, but all he was able to find was a huge, flat layer of stone in the ground, around 1,000 feet (305 m) by 800 feet (245 m), covered with sand and rock fragments. Was he looking in the wrong place? Or had this wonder of the ancient world been destroyed?

THE THEORIES

3 **IF THE LABYRINTH OF EGYPT** still exists, somewhere under the sands of Hawara, it would be a gold mine for Egyptologists. The carvings and inscriptions could include all kinds of new information and beautiful unknown artworks that could reveal more about the civilization that has captivated people's imaginations for centuries.

Petrie believed he had found what was left of the labyrinth. He thought the flat stone in the ground was the foundation or floor of the great building and the rest was gone. Egyptians often reused the stones from old ruins to make new buildings, so that's what the archaeologist thought had happened: The whole temple had been broken to bits and removed.

But had it? Several of those ancient writers agreed that the labyrinth had a huge roof, which seemed to be made from a single huge slab of stone. Was Petrie's stone "foundation" actually the roof of the labyrinth?

A PHARAOH HOLDS A CEREMONY IN A TEMPLE DEDICATED TO THE CROCODILE GOD SOBEK.

NEW EVIDENCE REVEALED!

IN 2008, a team of Egyptian and Belgian archaeologists organized a mission, known as the Mataha expedition, to take another look at the site. They couldn't dig into the ground, as a canal has been built through the area, making it waterlogged. Instead, they used ground-penetrating radar, which can scan under the ground to look for structures.

The scans revealed a thrilling new find. They showed a huge area of walls, rooms, and grid-like patterns built from some type of dense, strong stone. Could these be the ruins of the labyrinth itself? Until a full excavation can begin, we can only wait and wonder. Fingers crossed!

6

PERILOUS & PUZZLING PLACES

LONG AGO, people traveled the world in search of new lands they had never been to—or sometimes didn't even know existed. Many of these journeys were so far back in history that there's very little record of who went where and when. We have a handful of old maps, but even they can be curiously unreliable. Yet there is a scattering of strange evidence that suggests people were exploring and sailing around the world in ancient times, long before the age of exploration started in the 1400s.

Even into modern times, some parts of the world remained pristine and unexplored, or were unknown to outsiders—the deepest, most remote jungles and highest mountain peaks. Those who ventured into these unfamiliar realms sometimes never came back ... and what happened to them remains shrouded in mystery to this day.

The Atlantic Forest in Brazil

THE JUNGLE EXPLORER WHO MYSTERIOUSLY VANISHED

Experts think to this day there are native peoples living in the **AMAZON** rainforest who have never been contacted by the **OUTSIDE WORLD.**

The Amazon jungle is hot, dense, and crisscrossed by many rivers.

THE BACKGROUND

A SWASHBUCKLING BRITISH EXPLORER with a handlebar mustache braving the depths of the Amazon rainforest in search of a lost city named "Z"? It sounds like something from a comic book or a very cheesy movie. But this amazing adventure really happened.

Percy Fawcett first traveled to South America in 1906 to map a wild and remote part of the Amazon jungle. He went back several times, encountering giant snakes and spiders, befriending local rainforest peoples, and learning about the area.

Over the years, Fawcett heard rumors about a great city that had once existed there. He became obsessed with finding the ruins of the city, which he named Z. In 1925, he embarked on an expedition to look for it, taking his 21-year-old son, Jack, and Jack's friend Raleigh Rimell. Scientists and archaeologists thought Fawcett was crazy. But newspapers supported him, and he became very famous. The world waited to see if he would discover Z—and make it back alive.

Sadly, it wasn't to be. A few weeks after setting off, Fawcett wrote his wife a letter saying they were about to head into dangerous, unexplored territory. "You need have no fear of any failure," he reassured her. But the three men were never heard from again.

ATLANTIC OCEAN

Amazon River

BRAZIL

SOUTH AMERICA

PACIFIC OCEAN

■ Amazon Rainforest

PERCY FAWCETT FROM HIS FOURTH TRIP TO THE AMAZON

THE DETAILS

FAWCETT penned the letter to his wife on May 29, 1925. That was also the last time he, Jack, and Raleigh were seen before they disappeared. Shortly after, they set off into the unknown. The area they ventured into, in Brazil's Mato Grosso region, was home to many different native groups: some friendly to outsiders, and some not.

THE CLUES

When no one had heard from the trio for two years, several explorers and journalists set out to look for them—to no avail. The search has been on ever since. There are quite a few curious clues, but they don't all seem to add up!

PERCY'S BONES In 1951, Orlando Villas Bôas, an activist who worked to protect Brazil's native peoples, said that the Kalapalo people had told him that they had killed the three explorers. They had even given him Percy Fawcett's bones as proof. Case closed?

WE TOLD THEM NOT TO GO! In later interviews with the Kalapalo, they told a different story. They said they had warned the explorers not to continue, as hostile locals nearby would kill them. They carried on anyway, and the Kalapalo saw smoke from their campfires for the next five days. Then, nothing.

DON'T FOLLOW US! Fawcett said that if he went missing, no one should search for him, as it was too dangerous. It later turned out that some of the details he gave about where he was going were different from the plans found in his private diaries. Was he hiding something?

An artist's depiction of Percy Fawcett studying maps of the jungle to plan his route

THE THEORIES

IS THIS A MURDER MYSTERY, a tale of bad luck, or something stranger?

The remote Amazon rainforest is a dangerous place, and plenty of horrible things could have happened to Fawcett's group. They could have been eaten by jaguars, bitten by deadly snakes or spiders, or swept away in river rapids. They could have caught a killer disease from insect bites or ran out of food: These are all perfectly sensible theories.

FAWCETT IN BRAZIL

But what about those bones? They seem to have been a red herring. Later, another of Fawcett's sons, Brian, saw the bones. He found that the skeleton was shorter than his father and it had both its front teeth. But Percy Fawcett had false front teeth, as he had lost the real ones during childhood.

Could the explorers have been killed by a hostile group of people? This is possible, as some of the people in the area distrusted outsiders and often shot arrows at strangers. Fawcett always took a supply of gifts with him to help him make friends with people he met along the way. But the Kalapalo recounted that on his way to Dead Horse Camp, Fawcett had accidentally lost his gifts in a river, so had nothing left to offer.

But there's another possibility: that Fawcett survived. Some say he never actually planned to return; rather, he wanted to stay in the jungle permanently. There are even claims he planned to set up his own society, where locals would worship his son Jack as a god. There are several reports of sightings of an elderly Caucasian man being held prisoner by locals or wandering alone in the jungle.

Whatever happened, it seems that Percy Fawcett sadly didn't discover the lost city of Z. But maybe we have. In the early 2000s, satellite scanning technology revealed that there really are remains of ancient cities in the Amazon, now overgrown by jungle. So while we may never know what happened to him, Fawcett was probably right!

BOA CONSTRICTOR

IT'S **ON** THE MAP BUT IT **DOESN'T** EXIST!

The Icelandic island of **SURTSEY** first appeared in November 1963, formed by volcanic eruptions, and now it's **SHRINKING!**

Frisland

NORTH
AMERICA
EUROPE
ASIA
ATLANTIC
OCEAN
Hy-Brasil
L. Superior
INDIAN
OCEAN AUSTRALIA
PACIFIC
OCEAN
Emerald Island
ANTARCTICA

THE BACKGROUND

IF YOU LOOK at an old map of the world, you might be surprised to find some mysterious islands that aren't there today.

Take Frisland, a large island south of Iceland, shown on several maps from the 1500s and 1600s. With its many bays, headlands, and outlying smaller islands, it looks very realistic. It even has towns, with names like Ocibar, Godmec, and Cabaru. But there's actually no such place!

A famous 1755 map of North America, the Mitchell Map, shows four large islands in Lake Superior that don't exist. Then there's Emerald Island, south of New Zealand. It was put on the map after Captain William Elliot reported finding it in 1821 ... then it vanished!

And the little island of Hy-Brasil, off Ireland's west coast, appeared on maps from the 1300s to the 1800s, but it isn't really there. There were many legends about this peculiar place. People said it was home to a mysterious civilization, a group of saints, a wise old magician, or even a population of giant rabbits. According to Irish folklore, it was only visible for one day every seven years, and the rest of the time it was clouded in mist. Well, at least that would explain why it was so hard to find!

So what's going on with these strange places? Did mapmakers make mistakes, or did some areas actually vanish?

THE DETAILS

THESE ARE EXAMPLES OF "phantom islands": nonexistent landmasses that have appeared on maps throughout history. Hundreds of years ago, making maps wasn't easy. Mapmakers relied on previous maps and on reports from sailors and explorers, who were still discovering new lands. That's where most phantom islands seem to come from—but how, and why?

THE CLUES

Why would an island suddenly appear out of nowhere—or suddenly disappear? These clues might help!

→ **THE CLUE'S IN THE NAME** One of the phantom islands in Lake Superior was named Isle Philippeaux. Louis Phélypeaux was a wealthy French count who had paid for an explorer to investigate the area. Interesting ...

→ **NOW YOU SEE IT, NOW YOU DON'T!** In 1831, an island appeared in the Mediterranean Sea, south of Sicily, thanks to an underwater volcano erupting. By the following year, the sea had covered it. So an island *can* actually vanish!

→ **SEEING THINGS AT SEA** A mirage is an image of something that isn't really there, caused when layers of warm and cold air make light bend. Mirages often take the form of water that seems to be just out of reach in a hot desert, but they can happen at sea, too.

LOUIS PHÉLYPEAUX

THIS GLOBE FROM THE 1600S INCLUDES THE MADE-UP ISLAND OF FRISLAND.

THE THEORIES

ISLANDS REALLY CAN appear and disappear. Volcanoes can create brand-new land, and existing places can also vanish underwater. That very thing has been happening over the past 30 years, as rising seas have swallowed up several low-lying islands in the Pacific.

The oceans have risen in the past, too. That could explain the mystery of the Irish island Hy-Brasil. The place where it appeared on old maps was on a shallow sea. Perhaps the spot was once above the water's surface.

A ship sails past the newly formed volcanic island near Sicily in the year 1831.

Sailors and explorers often described islands they'd seen in the distance, without actually landing on them. A mirage at sea can look like cliffs or rocks on the horizon, when there's really nothing there. Faraway icebergs can also look like islands, especially around Antarctica, where Emerald Island was supposed to be.

However, a few phantom islands seem to have been total fakes. When the explorer Charlevoix published a map of Lake Superior, he added a generous sprinkling of islands and named them after his rich French patron and his lands, as a form of flattery. After all, His Excellency was never going to go and check, right?

As for Frisland, it first appeared on a map published in 1588 by Italian historian Nicolò Zeno. He claimed he had based it on letters and maps left by his ancestors, describing their travels in the 1300s. The map showed parts of North America: evidence, Zeno said, that his family had been the true discoverers of America.

Or not! Frisland was one of several phantom islands on the map, which strongly suggests that Zeno made this "evidence" up. But people at the time believed it and copied Frisland onto other maps for the next hundred years.

These days, you wouldn't get away with a hoax like that. Thanks to remote-sensing satellites, we can keep track of every part of the Earth—and no one gets to make up islands anymore!

HY-BRASIL

WHERE **IN** THE WORLD WAS THIS **WONDERFUL** LAND?

PHARAOH HATSHEPSUT

Hatshepsut's mortuary temple at Deir el-Bahari near the River Nile, where carvings show the details of the expedition to Punt

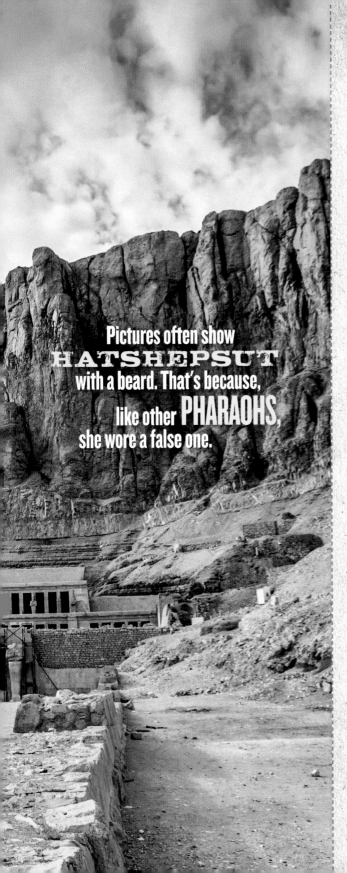

Pictures often show **HATSHEPSUT** with a beard. That's because, like other **PHARAOHS**, she wore a false one.

THE BACKGROUND

WHEN HATSHEPSUT BECAME PHARAOH of ancient Egypt around 3,500 years ago, she set out to show what a great and powerful leader she was. She built amazing temples and statues all over her kingdom, and she also organized a major trade mission.

Her target was the mysterious and fabulously wealthy Land of Punt. Egypt had traded with Punt before, but these trading trips had stopped. Hatshepsut wanted to revive them in a spectacular way and bring back boatloads of Punt's luxury goods: gold, ivory, ebony, perfume, makeup, and animal skins. This would help ensure prosperity and peace, impress her people, and also please the Egyptian god Amun. Hatshepsut had a fleet of five new ships built, and she loaded them with weapons, pottery, and minerals to trade with Punt. She sent Senenmut, her chief minister, to lead the trip, with more than one thousand sailors. It was a brilliant success, and the ships returned laden with treasures.

We know all this because Hatshepsut, like many pharaohs, built herself a temple for her tomb, ready for when she died. It was full of carved reliefs and inscriptions about her achievements, including the journey to Punt. It shows the ships, the voyage, the king and queen of Punt, and its houses and people, surrounded by tropical plants.

So we know what Punt was like, but to this day, experts aren't sure where it was. Some have asked if it even existed. If it did, where is it now?

THE DETAILS

THE RELIEFS IN Hatshepsut's temple show the ships setting off with river fish in the water, suggesting they sailed along the Nile. Later, according to the inscriptions, they reached the Red Sea. But where did they go from there? If the ships sailed down the Red Sea to reach it, Punt could have been on either the African side or the Arabian side of the Red Sea.

THE CLUES Archaeologists and historians have studied every detail they can find about Punt. Here are some of the clues they've considered.

➡ **THE LAND OF GOD** In some Egyptian writings, Punt was known as Ta netjer, "the land of God." This probably meant the land of the sun god, or the place where the sun rose: the east—meaning Punt was somewhere to the east of Egypt.

➡ **THOSE HOUSES ARE STILL THERE!** Though it was a long time ago, the round houses shown in the Punt reliefs are very similar to traditional huts, called tukuls, still found in the African countries of Sudan and Ethiopia.

➡ **LOOK TO THE WILDLIFE** The Punt reliefs also depict various plants and animals, including fish, leopards, giraffes, and apes. Could they help pin down the location?

THE THEORIES

ACCORDING TO some theories, Punt could be as far away as Indonesia, in Southeast Asia. Some say it was in what is now Israel, and the Egyptians actually sailed north to reach it. But most experts agree it must have been somewhere around the Red Sea.

At first, Punt was placed in Arabia, perhaps in what is now Yemen, thanks to the incense plants, such as myrrh, and the fish shown in the carvings. But later, theorists realized northeastern Africa was a better match. Not only does it have the same myrrh trees and fish, it also has all the animals in the Punt reliefs: the apes, leopards, monkeys, and giraffes. The trading mission brought back animal skins, and also living animals such as baboons, to be kept in temples or royal zoos.

Many historians today think Punt could have been in present-day Somalia, known for its incense, resins, and valuable aromatic woods, which the Egyptians prized. It's in the most easterly part of Africa, which would fit with the "land of God" name. And, in ancient times, the people of this area called their homeland "Bunn"—which sounds a little like "Punt."

But in 2010, scientists studied the DNA of an ancient baboon that had been brought back to Egypt from Punt as a pet, then preserved as a mummy. They found it was most closely related to baboons from Eritrea, which is north of Somalia—and right next to Ethiopia and Sudan, where there are tukuls similar to those in the Punt reliefs. So the mystery continues. Maybe Punt was big enough to include both areas. Maybe the baboon had migrated north. Or perhaps the location of Punt will remain Hatshepsut's secret forever.

TUKUL VILLAGE

MUMMIFIED BABOON

CARVING FROM THE TEMPLE OF HATSHEPSUT AT DEIR EL-BAHARI SHOWING MEN CARRYING A MYRRH TREE FOR SHIPMENT

AN ARTIST'S DEPICTION OF HATSHEPSUT RECEIVING GOODS FROM PUNT

An artist's depiction of the ships in which Columbus and his men crossed the Atlantic Ocean in the 1490s

According to old ICELANDIC sagas, or stories, Viking visitors to Canada fought battles with local native people, whom they called "SKRAELINGS."

IF IT **WASN'T** CHRISTOPHER COLUMBUS THEN JUST **WHO** WAS IT?

THE BACKGROUND

MANY THOUSANDS OF YEARS AGO, early humans spread out of Africa, across Asia, and up into Russia. They crossed into what is now Alaska, U.S.A.; when it was still linked to Russia by a bridge of land. From there, they moved south, becoming native North and South American peoples such as the Inuit, the Apache, the Aztec, and the Quechua.

But toward the end of the last ice age, around 11,000 years ago, the sea level rose and the land bridge was covered with water. America was cut off from Asia, Africa, and Europe, and it became much harder to cross the gap. Explorers from the rest of the world did not make contact with the Americas again until much, much later. Or so we think ...

You'll often hear that Christopher Columbus "discovered" America. He sailed across the Atlantic from Europe in 1492, landing in what is now the Bahamas. Though he never set foot on the North American mainland, he visited some Caribbean islands and the coasts of South and Central America. He's famous for being the first European to find the Americas.

But try telling that to the Vikings! More than 500 years before Columbus's first voyage, Viking sailors from Iceland settled in Greenland. From there, it wasn't far to North America, and several Viking voyages went there.

127

THE DETAILS

IN THE YEAR 986, Viking sailor Bjarni Herjólfsson was heading for Greenland when he was blown off course and spotted warmer lands to the south. Another Viking, Leif Eriksson, sailed in the same direction and landed in Newfoundland, Canada, which he called Vinland, around the year 1000. The Vikings didn't stay for long, but there's definite proof they were there. The remains of a Viking settlement can still be seen at L'Anse aux Meadows in Newfoundland. They also visited Labrador, on the Canadian mainland, which they called Markland. But who else made it to the Americas long before Columbus?

THE CLUES

There are actually all kinds of clues that point to others reaching the Americas even back into ancient times. Some are convincing, some not so much! Here are just a few of the continent-conquering contenders.

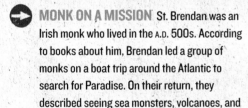

MONK ON A MISSION St. Brendan was an Irish monk who lived in the A.D. 500s. According to books about him, Brendan led a group of monks on a boat trip around the Atlantic to search for Paradise. On their return, they described seeing sea monsters, volcanoes, and a number of fabulous foreign lands.

POLYNESIAN POTATO PUZZLER Sweet potatoes are native to South America. But Polynesians from islands in the South Pacific have grown sweet potatoes since around A.D. 1000. And their name for them, *kuumala*, is almost the same as the South American Quechua name, *kumara*.

ARE THESE JAPANESE? Archaeologists have noticed that ancient pottery from Ecuador, in South America, looks strangely similar to the pottery of the Jōmon people from prehistoric Japan. Even weirder, some experts say that the native American Zuni language is similar to Japanese.

THE THEORIES

DID ANCIENT JAPANESE SAILORS take their pottery and language on a transpacific voyage? Did the Polynesians visit the Quechua and take some sweet potatoes home as a souvenir? And did an Irish monk really cross the Atlantic?

It might all sound pretty unlikely, but there's actually some evidence for all these theories. In modern times, storm winds and currents have swept several Japanese boats across the Pacific, some ending up close to California. We don't know if this happened in ancient times, too, but we do know it's possible. Some Japanese sailors could have survived a journey like this and moved in

ANCIENT HOMES OF VIKING SETTLERS AT L'ANSE AUX MEADOWS

POLYNESIAN BOAT

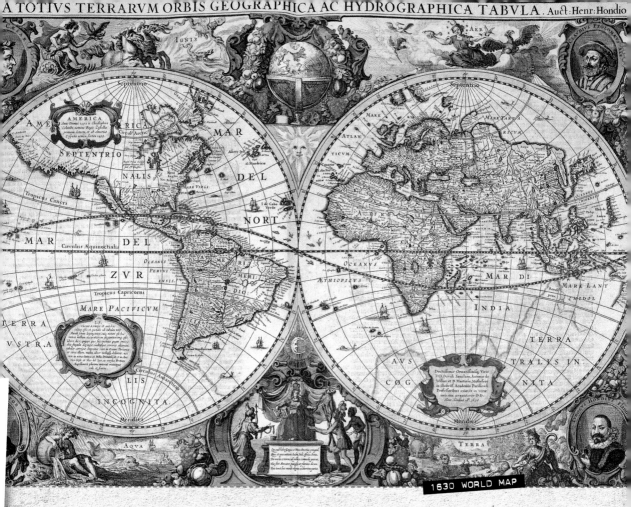

1630 WORLD MAP

with the locals, bringing their pottery styles and language with them.

And what about those Polynesian potatoes? Experts tested DNA from bits of sweet potato left behind on old Polynesian cooking pots and found the potatoes were indeed from South America, and they got there at least as early as A.D. 1000. Of course, it is possible that a potato could have made the journey by itself, floating across the sea. But experts think it's more likely the Polynesian sweet potatoes are evidence of early trade across the Pacific.

Finally, in 1976, explorer Tim Severin built a replica of a currach, the traditional boat that St. Brendan reportedly used for his adventure. Severin and his crew managed to sail it across

the Atlantic, with a stop in Iceland, all the way to Canada. And in West Virginia, U.S.A., archaeologists have found carvings that look like ogham, an ancient Irish alphabet. They could have been left there by ancient Irish explorers.

According to other theories, Africans, Phoenicians, and Arabs could also have paid the Americas a few early visits. It's hard to prove, but it's likely that at least one of these ancient adventuring peoples did make the trip. Sorry, Columbus— you were late!

JŌMON ERA POTTERY

GEORGE MALLORY

DID THEY MAKE IT
TO THE TOP OF EVEREST?

THE BACKGROUND

1 **IN 1921,** British mountaineers began a series of expeditions to try to climb Mount Everest, the world's highest mountain. A 1922 attempt failed, and so did one in 1924. Or did it?

During the 1924 expedition, three pairs of climbers tried to get to the top in separate attempts. The first two teams had to turn back—freezing temperatures, icy winds, and low oxygen levels made the task almost impossible. For the third attempt, experienced climber George Mallory chose young Andrew Irvine as his partner. They were friends, but Irvine was also good at repairing the basic oxygen tanks they used. This technology was new at the time, and the equipment often broke down, making Irvine's expertise essential for success.

On June 6, 1924, Mallory and Irvine set off from Camp 4, halfway up the mountain. By the next night, they had reached Camp 6, and they were ready to set off for the summit early in the morning.

On June 8, another team member, Noel Odell, thought he spotted the pair high up on Everest's Northeast Ridge through his binoculars. They were only around 800 feet (260 m) below the summit, near a steep crag known as the Second Step, and making for the top. But it was almost 1 p.m.—much later than planned.

Then clouds obscured the view, and it began snowing. Odell tried to call to Mallory and Irvine, but he heard no reply. They never returned.

THE DETAILS

2 **THERE'S NO WAY** the two men could have survived overnight so high up the mountain. The rest of the team knew they must have tragically died. But a major mystery remained: before disaster struck, did they reach the top of Everest, becoming the first people to climb it? Officially, Edmund Hillary and Tenzing Norgay became the first to scale Everest in 1953. But had Mallory and Irvine actually done it first, 29 years earlier? There were hardly any clues. In 1933, mountaineers found Irvine's ice ax some distance below the Second Step, and an oxygen cylinder from the expedition was found nearby in 1991. There were some possible sightings of the men's bodies. But several search parties failed to find them or their camera, which could reveal if they had stood on the summit.

THE THEORIES

3 **SOME CLIMBERS** think the men did reach the top. They might even have been on their way down when Odell spotted them and were backtracking a short way to take a photo.

Or, they could have perished on the way up, or abandoned the attempt and turned back, only to lose their way after darkness fell. The snowstorm Odell spotted would have made their climb incredibly cold and difficult. Some argue that their protective clothing and oxygen tanks, far more primitive than what modern climbers use, would have made it impossible for Mallory and Irvine to summit Everest at all. Today, a stone memorial commemorating their brave attempt stands at Everest's base camp.

ABOVE: Members of the 1924 expedition in a colorized photograph

LEFT: Mallory and Irvine

RIGHT: Mallory's pocket knife

NEW EVIDENCE REVEALED!

IN 1999, a team set out to look for the famous climbers' remains, or any equipment that might solve the mystery. Searching below the spot where the ice ax was found, they discovered a frozen body dressed in the clothing of the 1920s. As the ax was Irvine's, they expected it to be him, but it wasn't. It was George Mallory.

There was no camera with him, but his snow goggles were in his pocket. He had no oxygen with him, suggesting he had used it all. This could mean he had reached the top and was returning after sunset.

There was one more clue: Mallory had been carrying a photograph of his wife, Ruth, which he had planned to leave on the summit of Everest. It was not among the items found with his body. Perhaps it's still somewhere under the snow, at the top of Mount Everest.

VANISHING ACTS &
ASTONISHING
APPEARANCES

The remote Eilean Mor lighthouse, the scene of a famously spooky disappearance

THROUGHOUT HISTORY, a surprising number of people have vanished, never to be seen again. Often there's a simple explanation: They fell off a ship or got lost in a jungle. But there are some famously freaky cases that have never been solved. And it's not just mysterious disappearances that can be puzzling. Some people also seem to have appeared out of nowhere. Or both—as in the curious case of Gil Perez, who disappeared from one place and appeared in another, 9,000 miles (14,000 km) away, in the blink of an eye! (At least that's how he described it.)

When people strangely appear or disappear, it can quickly give rise to a range of rumors, legends, and spooky stories that try to explain the strange occurrence. But maybe a closer look at the clues in each case can lead us to the real reason it happened ... if there is one!

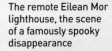

FAIRIES, ALIENS, OR GREEN CHILDREN?

THE BACKGROUND

IMAGINE YOU'RE A MEDIEVAL farmworker gathering crops in the fields, when suddenly you hear a strange sound, look up, and see two green children in front of you. Weird or what?

This is what happened in the village of Woolpit, in Suffolk, England, in the 1100s, according to local legends. The children, a boy and a girl, appeared in a field one day during harvesttime. They had green skin, spoke an unknown language, and seemed totally lost. Locals rescued them, and a wealthy landowner, Sir Richard de Caine, let them stay at his home.

At first, the children wouldn't eat anything, until someone brought them some freshly picked beans, which they grabbed and gobbled up. This seemed to be the only food they liked. Sadly, the boy passed away, but the girl, whom the villagers named Agnes, survived. Once she learned to speak English, she told a strange tale.

Agnes said that she and her brother had come from St. Martin's Land, a shadowy land with no sunlight where everyone was as green as them! They remembered watching over their cows and getting lost in a cave before finding themselves in the bright, sunny village.

Aliens are often described as
"LITTLE GREEN MEN."
Some say the idea could have come
from the story of Woolpit's
GREEN CHILDREN.

VILLAGE SIGN

The rural landscape where the children appeared

135

THE DETAILS

OK, IT MAY DATE BACK MORE THAN 800 years ago, but this eerie event is more than just an old village tale. It's actually found in two different medieval historical accounts. One is a record written by a monk who lived nearby around the year 1200. The other is a history of England written at about the same time. Both books tell the same story, with almost all the same details. Could it have really happened?

THE CLUES

Not much about this strange story seems to make sense. But if the green children were real, there are a few clues that might shed some light on who they were ...

GREEN NO MORE The children would only eat beans for weeks, but gradually they learned to eat other foods. As they did, they slowly lost their green skin color and looked healthier. Had the beans been turning them green ... or was it something else?

THE PITS OF WOOLPIT Woolpit was named for its wolf pits, holes dug in the ground to trap wolves that approached villages and keep people safe. The area also had many flint mines with underground passageways. Could these explain the "cave" that Agnes described?

CUT OFF BY A RIVER Agnes said that although St. Martin's Land was dark and gloomy, they had been able to see a brighter land in the distance, but they couldn't reach it because a big river lay in the way.

THE THEORIES

SOME SAY this must be just a fairy tale, passed on in gossip and hearsay until people believed it was true. But the details are so strange and specific that they don't seem made up. So historians have tried to figure out what could have really happened. Why were the children green? Why didn't they speak English, and where was the dimly lit St. Martin's Land?

Some say the children could have been poisoned. This could have made them look greenish from nausea, as well as very sick—perhaps this is why the boy died. When they tried new foods, they recovered.

What about their strange language? Historical evidence shows that in the 1100s, many Flemish people from Belgium migrated to Suffolk. According to one popular theory, the two children may have been Flemish orphans and ended up living wild in the forest. They only had wild plants to eat, which caused a type of malnutrition nicknamed "green sickness" for the green tinge it can give the victim's skin. Eventually, they wandered into the old flint mines, emerging near Woolpit.

And as for St. Martin's Land? It could have been Agnes's name for Fornham St. Martin, a nearby village, which was separated from the larger town by a river.

But hang on a moment—aren't we missing something? They were small, they were green: They could have been aliens! Yes, this explanation exists, too: One theory suggests the children could have accidentally teleported to Woolpit from their home planet.

In the end, Agnes, the surviving "green child," grew up in Woolpit and married a local. People say that her descendants still live there today. So, depending on which theory you believe, this English village could be home to part-alien beings!

AN ANCIENT WOLF TRAP IN THE MOUNTAINS OF NORTHERN SPAIN

COULD GREEN BEANS BE THE CULPRIT?

ST. MARY'S CHURCH IN WOOLPIT

WHO WAS THE WOMAN IN THE BIZARRE BOAT?

The appearance of a strange round boat on the shore of Japan baffled local fishermen.

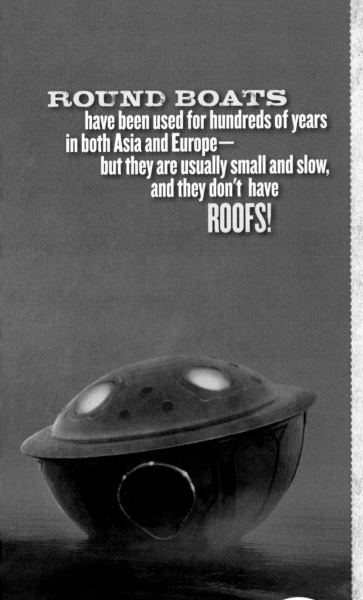

ROUND BOATS

have been used for hundreds of years in both Asia and Europe— but they are usually small and slow, and they don't have

ROOFS!

THE BACKGROUND

THE SCENE IS A FISHING VILLAGE in Hitachi, Japan, in the year 1803. At this time, Japan's rulers wanted to keep their country separate from the rest of the world and banned most foreigners from entering. So when a pale-skinned, red-haired stranger washed up in a weird-looking boat, you can imagine how surprised the locals were.

The story goes that some fishermen spotted a round boat in the waves and pulled it ashore. Unlike their own boats, this unusual vessel had a metal hull and a roof with clear windows. Its shape reminded people of a rice bowl or traditional incense burner. It's known as the "Utsuro-bune," or "hollow boat"— though in old drawings it looks more like a flying saucer!

The fishermen peered through the windows of the strange craft and spotted food and water, as well as unfamiliar writing on the walls. Then, to their amazement, they realized there was also a woman inside. She had light-colored skin, red hair with white ends, and clothes made from an unknown fabric. She spoke to the men, but no one understood her language.

According to the legend, the locals, unsure what to do with the woman, ended up putting her back into the boat and pushed her out to sea again. What became of her, no one knows...

ASIA
JAPAN

RUSSIA
NORTH KOREA
SOUTH KOREA
Sea of Japan
JAPAN
Hitachi
PACIFIC OCEAN

THE DETAILS

DESCRIPTIONS FROM old books about this strange encounter include plenty of details. They say the Utsuro-bune was about 18 feet (5.5 m) across by 11 feet (3.3 m) high. Its underside was made of metal plates, shown in a striped pattern in the drawings, and the windows were fixed into their frames with a soap-like substance. The accounts also describe the impossibly soft, smooth fabric of the woman's clothes, unlike anything the witnesses had seen before.

THE CLUES Is this eerie event a ludicrous legend or an unusual urban myth? Or is it a true story—and if so, who was this strange visitor? See what you think of these curious clues ...

MATCHING PICTURES In the years after 1803, when the hollow boat supposedly showed up, three different witnesses from the region wrote about it. They all included very similar information, as well as similar illustrations. Could this mean the accounts were based on a true story?

STRANGE INSCRIPTIONS Some of the accounts include copies of the mysterious markings found in the Utsuro-bune. They don't look like any writing we know of ... Or do they?

DON'T OPEN THE BOX! Besides her other possessions, the woman had a wooden box, which she clutched tightly at all times. She wouldn't let anyone go near it. What was all that about?

AN ARTIST'S DEPICTION THAT FOLLOWS OLD DESCRIPTIONS OF THE RED-HAIRED WOMAN AND HER STRANGE VESSEL

Other supposed UFO sightings seem eerily similar to the description of Utsuro-bune.

THE THEORIES

ACCORDING TO ONE of the descriptions, an old man in the village had his own theory about who the woman was. He reckoned she must be a princess from a foreign land who had fallen in love with a poor man. As punishment, the man had been executed, while the princess was cast out to sea in the boat. As for the box, he thought it must contain her boyfriend's head!

It sounds gruesome, but there are similar tales of secret boxes in several old Japanese folktales. And some say that's all this really is: folklore. They claim that the stories about it weren't in history books but storybooks, and the tale of Utsuro-bune is just a mishmash of old myths.

But what about all those weird details? Many Japanese folktales are about things like monsters and ghosts. The Utsuro-bune story isn't supernatural, but it does include very specific details about the woman's hair, possessions, and clothes, not to mention those weird symbols. This makes it seem more like a real-life unexplained event.

Another theory is that the stranger was Russian. Some Russians have red hair, and Russia was eager to start trading with Japan at the time. Could the woman have been a spy on a scouting mission (in a very bizarre boat)?

Or was she actually an alien? Some ufologists claim the Utsuro-bune was a flying saucer that had crash-landed in the sea. It doesn't just look like one; there's also another piece of eerie evidence that supports this out-of-this-world theory. In 1980, people reported spotting a UFO in Rendlesham Forest in Suffolk, England. Eyewitnesses sketched the strange symbols they saw on it ... and they're spookily similar to those in the Utsuro-bune. Could this be a language from another planet? If so, we just need to figure out what it means so we can chat with the aliens the next time they visit!

THE SPOOKY STORY OF THE TELEPORTING PALACE GUARD

VINOTERIA

142

In 2017, scientists successfully **TELEPORTED** a tiny particle called a **PHOTON** from Earth to a satellite 300 miles (483 km) away in space.

THE BACKGROUND

TELEPORTATION, or moving in an instant over a long distance, happens in sci-fi movies as a handy form of transportation. But although we may dream of how useful it could be, no one has yet invented a way for us to do it.

However, there is an account of real-life teleportation, dating from over 400 years ago: the strange case of Gil Perez. Unlike sci-fi space travelers, Perez didn't teleport on purpose. According to the story, it just happened to him without warning one day in October 1593.

Perez was a Spanish soldier in Manila, the modern-day capital of the Philippines. In those days, the Philippines, like several other parts of the world, was ruled by Spain. The Spanish governor had a palace in Manila, and Perez was a guard there. But the day before the strange event occurred, the governor had been murdered on an expedition, and the guards were waiting for a new governor to be appointed. Feeling tired, Perez leaned against a wall and closed his eyes for a moment. And when he opened them ... he was no longer in Manila!

He didn't know where he was, but local guards soon spotted the soldier in the unfamiliar uniform and challenged him. To Perez's amazement, they told him he was in Mexico City. This was also part of Spain's empire—but some 9,000 miles (14,000 km) away from Manila!

ASIA

Manila, Philippines

NORTH AMERICA

PACIFIC OCEAN

SOUTH AMERICA

AUSTRALIA

Mexico City, Mexico

Mexico City's Plaza Mayor, where Gil Perez unexpectedly found himself after disappearing from Manila

THE DETAILS

WHEN PEREZ EXPLAINED what had happened, the Mexican guards—unsurprisingly—thought he was insane. But Perez did seem to know a lot about the Philippines, and he also told them the news about the murder of the governor. The guards arrested him, and he was thrown into jail—for deserting his post in Manila, and, if what he said was true, for being involved in some kind of witchcraft. Poor old Perez could only insist that he'd closed his eyes in one part of the world and opened them in another, "in less time than it takes a cock to crow."

THE CLUES
It might seem impossible, and it certainly did to the authorities in Mexico, but eventually, more clues arrived to back up what Perez had said.

THE GOVERNOR IS DEAD! Two months after Perez had appeared so suddenly, a ship arrived in Mexico from the Philippines. As there were no phones or email then, it brought the news of the Manila governor's death, just as Perez had described. This was the first evidence that Perez was telling the truth. He was then allowed to sail back to Manila.

I RECOGNIZE THAT GUARD ... One of the sailors on the ship even recognized Perez, and he said that he had seen him in Manila not long before the day he turned up in Mexico.

TELEPORTATION TESTS But can teleportation actually happen? Kind of! Since the 1990s, scientists have been able to perform a basic type of teleportation, using tiny particles and re-creating them in a new location without actually moving them. That's a long way from zapping a palace guard across the globe, but it does show that teleportation is possible in theory.

THE THEORIES

THIS IS ONE BIZARRE mystery from history that's certainly going to take some explaining. There are several theories about it, but they are mostly pretty hard to swallow.

The first, but freakiest, theory is that Gil Perez actually did teleport 9,000 miles (14,000 km) in a few seconds, for some unknown reason, accidentally, and without the help of a single scientist. That could only happen if there are some strange aspects of science we don't yet understand.

Some people have suggested another idea: Perez was drawn through some kind of wormhole or energy field focused on Mexico City. Some people believe this ancient city has mystical powers, which is why the Aztec built their capital there, long before the Spanish invaded.

It's all very exciting, but sadly lacking in solid evidence. A more down-to-earth explanation is that although the story seems to be historical, it may be mostly hearsay. Though it's well known and reported in several old books, there are no really reliable records from the time it's said to have happened. Is it just an urban legend that's been spun into a spooky sci-fi story over the years?

We can't be sure, but it does seem more likely than the other theories. However, don't give up on teleportation just yet! Scientists are still working on it, and one day we could all be zapping around the globe, just like Gil Perez.

WHAT WOULD IT FEEL LIKE TO TRAVEL ACROSS THE WORLD IN AN INSTANT?

Gil Perez puzzles the
religious authorities
during questioning.

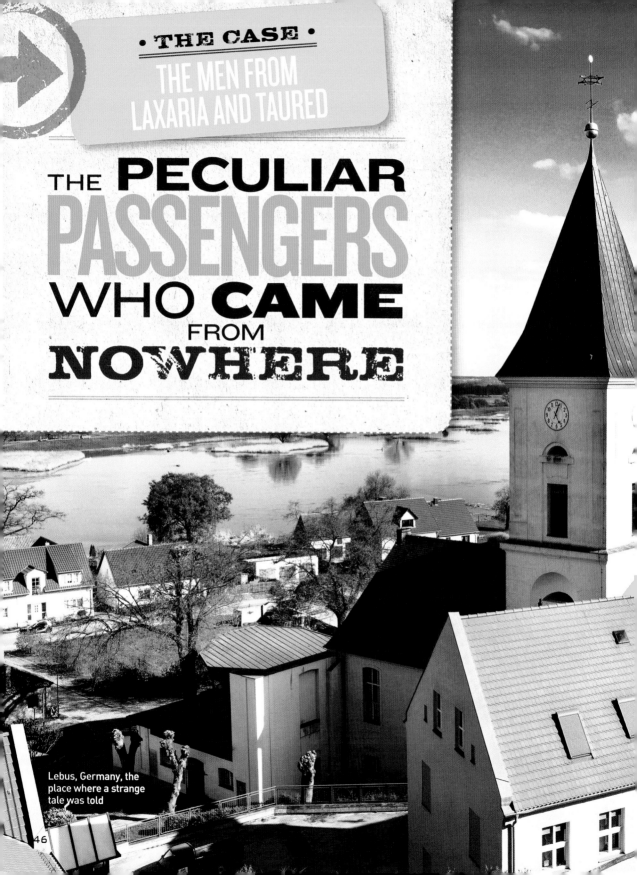

• THE CASE •

THE MEN FROM LAXARIA AND TAURED

THE PECULIAR PASSENGERS WHO CAME FROM NOWHERE

Lebus, Germany, the place where a strange tale was told

Many scientists, including the great physicist **STEPHEN HAWKING**, have said that **TIME TRAVEL** is scientifically possible.

THE BACKGROUND

IMAGINE MEETING SOMEONE from a place you'd never heard of. Well, that could happen. But what if it was a place that no one had ever heard of, and that wasn't on any map? That's what happened in these bizarre mysteries.

As the story goes, in 1954, a man arrived at Haneda Airport in Tokyo, Japan. When passport control asked where he was from, he said, "Taured." The airport employees were confused—because no such country existed. So the traveler showed them his passport, marked with the country name Taured. It even had airport stamps in it showing he had visited Japan before! He claimed Taured was between France and Spain and had existed for a thousand years.

The staff kept the man's passport and put him up in a hotel overnight while they investigated. But in the morning, the man had vanished … and so had his passport!

There's a similar story from Lebus, Germany, from 1851. A strange man was found in the streets and taken to the mayor. In poor German, he explained his name was Jophar Vorin and he was from Laxaria, in the continent of Sakria, far away across the sea. But neither Laxaria nor Sakria are real places. So what on Earth was going on?

THE DETAILS

WHEN BAFFLED OFFICIALS asked the man from Taured to show them his country on a map, he pointed to Andorra, a small country between France and Spain. He was angry that it was marked Andorra, though, as he insisted it was called Taured.

The man from Laxaria, however, claimed he had been in a shipwreck during his journey. When he was shown a globe, he was unable to point out his route or his homeland.

THE CLUES These accounts are certainly very odd, and there aren't many clues as to what was going on. But take a closer look ...

LOCAL LANGUAGES Despite coming from unknown lands, these travelers had no trouble speaking to locals. The man from Taured spoke both French and fluent Japanese. And the man from Laxaria could speak German, although he wasn't very good at it.

VANISHED WITHOUT A TRACE It would be handy if these mysterious men had stuck around to help investigators get to the bottom of the mystery. Instead, they seem to have disappeared, along with the Taured man's paperwork.

CONTINENTS OF THE WORLD Besides explaining that his homeland was on the continent of Sakria, the man from Laxaria named the other continents of the world as he knew them. They were Aflar, Aslar, Auslar, and Euplar. Sound familiar?

THE THEORIES

WHAT WAS REALLY HAPPENING in these curious cases? There are certainly some wacky theories out there. One is that the men had traveled through time, from a future when countries and continents have different names.

Or perhaps they came from other universes. The "multiverse" is one theory from physics that suggests there could be countless universes, all different from each other. Some would be similar to our own—so, for example, other Earths could have the same continents but with different names. The theory doesn't say people can travel between the universes, but some people say this is what must have happened here. Maybe the men popped through a wormhole or some other unknown link between one universe and another.

Perhaps the confusion happened because the travelers came from a future or a different

ANDORRA

universe in which these continent names were slightly different. The name "Taured" sounds a little like the "-dorra" part of Andorra. And the continent names given by the man from Laxaria are comparable to the names of some of Earth's continents: Aflar, Aslar, Auslar, and Euplar are similar to Africa, Asia, Australia, and Europe.

Or, the men simply could have had some kind of illness or amnesia that left them confused. Or perhaps these mysterious events were deliberate hoaxes.

The truth is, it's quite hard to know how reliable these reports really are. You can find the man from Taured all over the internet, but when you try to track down the original source, the trail goes cold. The story first appeared more than 20 years after 1954, in a book about mysterious events. Without the internet, it might have remained there. Now something that might have been made up can be quickly copied around the internet until it's seen as true.

The visit of Jophar Vorin of Laxaria was reported in several magazines soon after it happened, making it a little more convincing. But we still have no idea where the mysterious men really came from: space, the future, or somewhere else?

WHAT BECAME OF THE THREE MISSING LIGHTHOUSE KEEPERS?

THE BACKGROUND

1 **IN THE DARK AND STORMY** December of 1900, the steamship *Archtor* was crossing the Atlantic from Philadelphia, U.S.A., to Edinburgh, Scotland. As it passed the remote Flannan Isles, the captain saw that the newly built lighthouse on Eilean Mor had gone dark.

When a supply boat sailed to the island on December 26, the crew found the lighthouse deserted. A chair in the kitchen was overturned. The clocks had stopped, and only one of the lighthouse keepers' waterproof coats was there: The other two were gone. Entries in the logbook said there had been severe storms, which had damaged some equipment. But the last entry, on December 15, said the storm was over. The crew searched all around the island, but the three lighthouse keepers, Thomas Marshall, James Ducat, and Donald McArthur, had vanished.

LIGHTHOUSE LAMP

THE DETAILS

2 **THE COLD, LONELY FLANNAN ISLES** lie 75 miles (120 km) off the Scottish mainland. In 1900, they were uninhabited, apart from the three keepers. Even Eilean Mor, the largest island, was little more than a tall rock edged by cliffs. It wasn't a welcoming place to work—and to make matters worse, people nearby believed the islands were cursed. Also known as the Seven Hunters, the islands were said to be haunted by a spooky ghost ship, as well as a mysterious being known as the Phantom of the Seven Hunters. Yikes!

THE THEORIES

3 **AS WITH SO MANY** spooky stories, there is no shortage of unbelievable theories about what

might have happened. The three keepers could have been kidnapped by the ghostly ship or cursed to drown by the phantom, who didn't want anyone living there. Or maybe they were captured by pirates or escaped aboard a passing ship to get away from the eerie islands. Or perhaps they were carried away in the claws of a monstrous seabird or in the jaws of a giant sea serpent or—of course—abducted by an alien spaceship.

Eilean Mor's lonely lighthouse is surrounded by dangerous cliffs.

There were also some more reasonable suggestions. One of the men, McArthur, was known to be troublesome. Had he fallen out with the others, killed them, then escaped or drowned? Or perhaps the keepers were all simply washed away by a big wave. But this shouldn't have been possible, as there were strict rules that at least one man had to be in the lighthouse at all times. And why would there be storm waves when the logbook said the storm had ended? The mystery has endured for more than a century.

NEW EVIDENCE REVEALED!

IN RECENT YEARS, researchers have studied every detail of the story to try to find the answer. The latest theories return to the idea of a wave ... but not just any wave. In 1995, for the first time, scientists confirmed proof of huge "rogue" waves, which appear out of the sea with no warning. Once thought to be no more than sailors' tales, these huge waves, much larger than those around them, were finally proved to exist when measuring devices on an offshore oil platform detected one. More recently, a survey ship encountered a massive 95-foot (29 m)-tall rogue wave near Scotland. Had a wave like this struck the Flannan Isles?

Maybe after the big storm had died down, two of the keepers went out to fix damaged equipment, wearing their coats. The third, left to guard the lighthouse, saw the huge wave approaching and rushed out in a hurry to warn the others—only for all three of them to be swept away. If so, a monster wave like that would have been scarier than any ghost!

INTERVIEW

DIGGING TO SOLVE MYSTERIES
WITH
DR. EVA MOL

WHEN SHE WAS A CHILD, Eva Mol kept collections of rocks and fossils. Later on, she followed her passion for the past and became an archaeologist. She now teaches archaeology at Brown University in Providence, Rhode Island, U.S.A., and excavates ancient sites in Rome, Italy. She's especially interested in the connections between ancient artifacts, myths, and folklore. Read on to find out what digging deep to uncover history's mysteries is really like!

A DAY ON SITE. Most of the time I work at the university, writing, thinking, reading, and teaching. But sometimes I work at a Roman site in Molise in Italy, where a typical day starts at six in the morning. We work slowly in the

DR. MOL IN CYPRUS

burning sun, uncovering the past layer by layer, with trowels and pickaxes. We document everything we find—drawing, measuring, and taking pictures. After lunch and a siesta [an afternoon nap], we wash the finds, often hundreds of them: things like pottery fragments, tiles, and bricks. We record what we did that day in a database. At around 8 we have dinner, and at 11 or 12 I collapse on my bed. In the morning, the alarm buzzes at 5:30 again!

Some of the ancient ruins at Molise in Italy

PIECES OF THE PUZZLE. Working on an excavation is like trying to solve a large and complex puzzle. You are a detective, carefully disentangling and studying the smallest pieces of evidence. You have to figure out what happened long ago from just a few clues: a piece of pottery, an earring, a fragment of sculpture, a lamp. Was this site an ancient temple or a farmstead? Who lived here? How does the site relate to what we think we know from history? When you connect the dots, it's a great feeling.

TOUCHING THE PAST. I almost constantly think about the people who used and made things, and how these objects affected their lives. Even though these people were pretty different from me, I do have moments when I feel a deep connection between people in the past and myself: for instance, when I find fingerprints on an object. Suddenly you realize that millennia ago, someone was making this object, pressing his or her fingers into the clay under the same sun. Who else but this person, and now me, has paid that much attention to this object? Probably just the two of us.

OBJECTS AND STORIES. I am especially interested in how ancient myths connect to culture. How do some objects and landscapes create stories that people believe in? The Trojan horse, the Hut of Romulus, Atlantis ... why do we think these existed? Archaeology has a special role in the understanding of myths, legends, and folklore, because both archaeology and myth are ways to explain what happened in the past.

HISTORY AND MYSTERY. What if we could suddenly prove, once and for all, that Stonehenge was, let's say, an ancient sundial? The mystery would be solved for good. Wouldn't that be a bit disappointing? I think it is important that some mysteries remain, to inspire us to wonder about the world beyond what we see.

COULD YOU DO IT, TOO? My advice for anyone who'd like to be an archaeologist is to read a lot of books, and to visit museums and excavations if you can. Always question everything you read, see, and hear: Why do people make certain statements about the past, what are their arguments, and how did they get their answers? Besides that, you should never lose the power of wonder, curiosity, and imagination—there is still a lot to discover!

AFTERWORD

OLD FAIRY TALES, folklore, and legends might seem to be little more than made-up myths, but as this book reveals, there's often some real-life history lurking behind those old stories. The more mysterious monuments, curious carvings, buried bones, and amazing ancient artwork we find, the better we can piece together what really went on in the past. And the most exciting thing is, there's still so much more to discover! Thanks to new hi-tech methods, experts are unearthing new evidence all the time. Will we ever get to the bottom of all the mysteries history has to offer? Maybe not ... but one thing's for sure: We'll never stop exploring them!

ANCIENT ROMAN RUINS
OF A TEMPLE AT BAALBEK

INDEX

INDEX

INDEX

ILLUSTRATION CREDITS

COVER: Panther Media GmbH/ASP; (LO RT), Kumar Sriskandan/ASP; (labyrinth), Cegli/SS; (ax), PNC Collection/ASP; (mermaid), solarseven/SS; (alien), adike/SS; (tag), Andrey_Kuzmin/SS; **BACK COVER:** (UP), Zzvet/SS; (CTR), Private Collection/Look and Learn/BI; (LO), Dale O'Dell/ASP; **FRONT MATTER:** 1 (paper), paladin13/iStockPhoto/GI; 1, Macrovector/SS; 2 (CTR LE) Jim Richardson/GI; 2 (CTR RT), Private Collection/BI; 2 (LO CTR), George Steinmetz/GI; 2 (LO LE), Private Collection/Look and Learn/BI; 2 (LO RT), Hauke Vagt; 2 (UP CTR), Chris A Crumley/ASP; 2 (UP LE), Naturfoto Honal/GI; 2 (UP RT), ullstein bild/GI; 3 (LO), Monik-a/SS; 3 (UP), Amanda Lewis/GI; 5 (CTR), Historic Images/ASP; 5 (UP), Anton_Ivanov/SS; **CHAPTER 1:** 7 (LO), Grant Dixon/GI; 7 (CTR), HWitte/SS; 8-9 (CTR), Pictures from History/BI; 10-11 (CTR), Dinodia Photos/ASP; 11 (LO), John Elk III/GI; 12 (LO), Universal Images Group North America LLC/ASP; 12 (UP), Private Collection/The Stapleton Collection/BI; 13 (UP), British Library, London, UK/British Library Board. All Rights Reserved/BI; 15 (CTR), Private Collection/Look and Learn/BI; 16 (LO), Chris Howes/Wild Places Photography/ASP; 17 (CTR), Private Collection/Look and Learn/BI; 18 (CTR), Pictures from History/BI; 18-19 (CTR), Private Collection/Photo Christie's Images/BI; 20 (LO), British Museum/Universal History Archive/UIG/BI; 20-21 (CTR), Victoria & Albert Museum, London, UK/Ann & Bury Peerless Picture Library/BI; 21 (LO), Private Collection/The Stapleton Collection/BI; 21 (UP), petpics/ASP; 22-23 (paper), Rouzes/GI; 22-23 (ALL), roonzography/SS; **CHAPTER 2:** 24-25, Chris A Crumley/ASP; 26-27, Andrea Izzotti/SS; 27 (UP), Private Collection/Look and Learn/BI; 28-29, Brian J. Skerry/NGIC; 28, Historical Images Archive/ASP; 29, Universitatsbibliothek, Heidelberg, Germany/BI; 30-31, Coneyl Jay/GI; 32 (UP), Historic Images/ASP; 32 (LO), Naturfoto Honal/GI; 33, Chien Lee/Minden Pictures; 34-35 (CTR), whitemay/GI; 36 (UP), Bettmann/GI; 37 (ALL), Private Collection/Look and Learn/BI; 38-39, SinghaphanAllB/GI; 38 (LO), Ivan Mackerle; 41 (RT), Alexander Tomlinson; 41 (LO LE), Ivan Mackerle; 41 (CTR LE), Natural Visions/ASP; 43, Katie Barker/EyeEm/GI; 44, Sandra Mansi/Courtesy of ECHO, Leahy Center for Lake Champlain; 45, MichaelTaylor3d/SS; 46-47, MIXA/GI; 47 (LO), Philipp Zechner/ASP; 48-49 (UP), Pictures from History/BI; 48-49 (LO), The History Collection/ASP; 49, Cyril Ruoso/Minden Pictures; 50, Paul D. Stewart/Science Source; 51, NGIC; **CHAPTER 3:** 52-53, Hoiseung Jung/EyeEm/GI; 54-55, nudiblue/GI; 55 (UP), Brandelet/SS; 56 (LO), Nature Picture Library/ASP; 57 (UP), Hoiseung Jung/EyeEm/GI; 57 (LO), Chris Willson/ASP; 58-59, John Stanmeyer/VII; 58 (INSET), Barcroft/GI; 60 (UP), Bradley Russell; 60 (LO), Paul Nicklen/NGIC; 61, Rait Kütt; 62-63, ehrlif/GI; 62 (INSET), Tane Casserley/NOAA/Museum of Anthropological Archaeology, University of Michigan; 64-65 (ALL), Mark Holley; 66, Hauke Vagt; 67, Manfred Schmid/GI; **CHAPTER 4:** 68-69, George Steinmetz/GI; 70-71 (CTR), daverhead/GI; 70 (INSET), SuziMcGregor/GI; 72 (UP), sumikophoto/SS; 72 (LO), Duby Tal/Albatross/ASP; 73 (UP), Chr. Offenberg/SS; 73 (LO), DEA/G.Dagli Orti/GI; 74-75, James Thompson/ASP; 76-77, Fulcanelli/SS; 77 (UP), Alice Heart/SS; 77 (LO), alanfin/GI; 78-79, mountainpix/SS; 78 (UP), adike/SS; 80, Grant Dixon/GI; 81 (UP), Colin D. Young/SS; 81 (LO), George Steinmetz/GI; 82-83, NASA/JPL/Arizona State University/Science Photo Library/GI; 84 (ALL), NASA/JPL-Caltech; 85 (ALL), NASA/JPL-Caltech/Univ. of Arizona; 86-87, DEA/G.SIOEN/GI; 88-89, Amanda Lewis/GI; 89, Valley of the Kings, Thebes, Egypt/BI; 90, Natalia Bratslavsky/SS; 91, Norris RD, Norris JM, Lorenz RD, Ray J, Jackson B; **CHAPTER 5:** 92-93, Monik-a/SS; 94-95, Richard Yoshida/SS; 94 (INSET), Eva Mont/SS; 96, Richard Yoshida/SS; 97, George F. Mobley/NGIC; 98 (UP), VectorStock.com; 99, Private Collection/Look and Learn/BI; 100 (UP), Neirfy/SS; 100 (LO), DEA/A. De Gregorio/GI; 100 (axe), PNC Collection/ASP; 101, Pecold/SS; 102-105 (ALL), Vincent J. Musi/NGIC; 106-107, ullstein bild/GI; 108 (UP), Jens Schlueter/GI; 108 (LO), ullstein bild/GI; 109 (UP), Frank Ellmerich/GI; 109 (CTRRT), State Museum of Prehistory, Halle, Germany/BI; 110, Granger Historical Picture Archive/ASP; 111, Stefano Bianchetti/GI; **CHAPTER 6:** 112-113, FG Trade/GI; 114-115, apomares/GI; 115, Granger Historical Picture Archive/ASP; 116, Private Collection/Look and Learn/BI; 117 (UP), Royal Geographical Society, London, UK/BI; 117 (LO), Matt Jeppson/SS; 118-119, WeiseMaxHelloween/GI; 120-121, Art Collection 2/ASP; 120 (UP), Photo Collection Gregoire/BI; 120 (LO), Private Collection/Photo Christie's Images/BI; 121, David Neikirk/University of Southern Maine; 122-123, donvictorio/GI; 122 (INSET), Egyptian National Museum, Cairo, Egypt/BI; 124 (LE), Daniel Simon/GI; 124 (RT), ICHAUVEL/GI; 125 (UP), Kenneth Garrett/NGIC; 125 (LO), NGIC; 126-127, Private Collection/BI; 128 (UP), George Burba/SS; 128 (LO), Herbert Kane/NGIC; 129 (UP), Private Collection/BI; 129 (LO), Robert and Lisa Sainsbury Collection/BI; 130, Royal Geographical Society/GI; 131 (UP RT), Private Collection/Prismatic Pictures/BI; 131 (LO RT), Jim Fagiolo/Mallory & Irvine/GI; 131 (LO LE), Royal Geographical Society/GI; **CHAPTER 7:** 132-133, Paul Williams/ASP; 134-135, Matt Garbutt/EyeEm/GI; 135 (LO), Ros Drinkwater/ASP; 137 (UP), Ashley Cooper/ASP; 137 (CTR), SOMMAI/SS; 137 (LO), Robert Estall photo agency/ASP; 138-140 (ALL), Antonio Caparo 141, geogphotos/ASP; 142-143, The Picture Art Collection/ASP; 144, Engin Sezer/ASP; 145, Frank E. Schoonover Fund; 146-147, Ulf Boettcher/GI; 148-149, Mlenny/GI; 150, Universal History Archive/UIG/BI; 151, Paul Williams/ASP; **BACK MATTER:** 152, Ian J Cohn; 153, Universal Images Group North America LLC/DeAgostini/ASP; 154-155, Milonk/SS; 160, Jim Richardson/NGIC

CREDITS

For Bex —AC

Since 1888, the National Geographic Society has funded more than 12,000 research, exploration, and preservation projects around the world. The Society receives funds from National Geographic Partners, LLC, funded in part by your purchase. A portion of the proceeds from this book supports this vital work. To learn more, visit natgeo.com/info.

NATIONAL GEOGRAPHIC and Yellow Border Design are trademarks of the National Geographic Society, used under license.

For more information, visit nationalgeographic.com, call 1-800-647-5463, or write to the following address:

National Geographic Partners
1145 17th Street N.W.
Washington, D.C. 20036-4688 U.S.A.

Visit us online at nationalgeographic.com/books

For librarians and teachers: ngchildrensbooks.org

More for kids from National Geographic: kids.nationalgeographic.com

National Geographic Kids magazine inspires children to explore their world with fun yet educational articles on animals, science, nature, and more. Using fresh storytelling and amazing photography, *Nat Geo Kids* shows kids ages 6 to 14 the fascinating truth about the world—and why they should care. **kids.nationalgeographic.com/subscribe**

For information about special discounts for bulk purchases, please contact National Geographic Books Special Sales: specialsales@natgeo.com

For rights or permissions inquiries, please contact National Geographic Books Subsidiary Rights: bookrights@natgeo.com

Art directed by Kathryn Robbins
Designed by James Hiscott, Jr.

The publisher would like to thank the team who helped make this book possible: Ariane Szu-Tu, editor; Stephanie Warren Drimmer, project editor; Sarah J. Mock, senior photo editor; Joan Gossett, editorial production manager; Gus Tello and Anne LeongSon, design production assistants; and Scott Vehstedt, fact-checker.

Library of Congress Cataloging-in-Publication Data

Names: Claybourne, Anna, author.
Title: History's mysteries : legend and lore/by Anna Claybourne. Other titles: Legend and lore
Description: Washington, DC : National Geographic Kids, [2019] | Audience: Ages 8-12. | Audience: Grades 4-6.
Identifiers: LCCN 2018035849| ISBN 9781426334634 (hardcover) | ISBN 9781426334627 (paperback)
Subjects: LCSH: Legends--Juvenile literature. | History--Miscellanea--Juvenile literature.
Classification: LCC GR78 .C55 2019 | DDC 398.2--dc23
LC record available at https://lccn.loc.gov/2018035849

Printed in Malaysia
19/IVM/1